Advanced Sciences and Technologies for Security Applications

Indexed by SCOPUS

The series Advanced Sciences and Technologies for Security Applications comprises interdisciplinary research covering the theory, foundations and domain-specific topics pertaining to security. Publications within the series are peer-reviewed monographs and edited works in the areas of:

- biological and chemical threat recognition and detection (e.g., biosensors, aerosols, forensics)
- crisis and disaster management
- terrorism
- cyber security and secure information systems (e.g., encryption, optical and photonic systems)
- traditional and non-traditional security
- energy, food and resource security
- economic security and securitization (including associated infrastructures)
- transnational crime
- human security and health security
- social, political and psychological aspects of security
- recognition and identification (e.g., optical imaging, biometrics, authentication and verification)
- smart surveillance systems
- applications of theoretical frameworks and methodologies (e.g., grounded theory, complexity, network sciences, modelling and simulation)

Together, the high-quality contributions to this series provide a cross-disciplinary overview of forefront research endeavours aiming to make the world a safer place.

The editors encourage prospective authors to correspond with them in advance of submitting a manuscript. Submission of manuscripts should be made to the Editor-in-Chief or one of the Editors.

More information about this series at http://www.springer.com/series/5540

Cindy Vestergaard
Editor

Blockchain for International Security

The Potential of Distributed Ledger
Technology for Nonproliferation and Export
Controls

 Springer

Editor
Cindy Vestergaard
Stimson Center
Washington, DC, USA

ISSN 1613-5113   ISSN 2363-9466 (electronic)
Advanced Sciences and Technologies for Security Applications
ISBN 978-3-030-86242-8   ISBN 978-3-030-86240-4 (eBook)
https://doi.org/10.1007/978-3-030-86240-4

This Springer imprint is published by the registered company Springer Nature Switzerland AG
The registered company address is: Gewerbestrasse 11, 6330 Cham, Switzerland

Acknowledgements

This volume is a collection of chapters by experts who represent a small but growing group of researchers who are studying distributed ledger technology (DLT) and its potential to create greater efficiencies and effectiveness in data management and information sharing related to international security. Their work is lacing new trails by investigating and testing the tech in ways that allow for independent analysis which is made public and available to the international non-proliferation community. I am indebted to them for these efforts as they have advanced our knowledge on the potential for DLT and non-proliferation. I am also grateful to them for their collaboration on this book, particularly for their flexibility and patience as the COVID-19 global pandemic messed with deadlines and response times. A shout out to all authors and to Gabrielle Green's ruthless review of draft texts. Special dedication also goes to Sarah Frazar and Andrea Viski for stepping in when I needed help the most. I am also grateful to the Carnegie Corporation of New York (CCNY) for their generous support in funding a portion of this research and to Springer for their support in publishing the book.

Cindy Vestergaard

Contents

Contributors

Haimanot Anbesaw Bobosha The Henry L. Stimson Center, Washington, DC, USA

Richard T. Cupitt The Henry L. Stimson Center, Washington, DC, USA

Diego Cándano Laris The Henry L. Stimson Center, Washington, DC, USA

Sarah Frazar Global Security Technology and Policy Group, Pacific Northwest National Laboratory, Seattle, WA, USA

Karolin Langfeldt Circulor, London, USA

Edward Obbard School of Mechanical and Manufacturing Engineering, University of New South Wales, Kensington, Australia

Guntur Dharma Putra School of Computer Science and Engineering, University of New South Wales, Kensington, Australia

Maria Lovely Umayam Venice, CA, USA;
The Henry L. Stimson Center, Washington, DC, USA

Cindy Vestergaard The Stimson Center, Washington, DC, USA

Edward Yu School of Mechanical and Manufacturing Engineering, University of New South Wales, Kensington, Australia

Abbreviations

A/CPPNM	Amended Convention for the Physical Protection of Nuclear Material
ANSTO	Australian Nuclear Science and Technology Organisation
AP	Additional Protocol
API	Application Programming Interface
ASNO	Australian Safeguards and Nonproliferation Office
ATT	Arms Trade Treaty
BFT	Byzantine Fault Tolerance
BIS	Bureau of Industry and Security
CAS	Chemical Abstracts Service
CPPNM	Convention on the Physical Protection of Nuclear Material
CSA	Comprehensive Safeguards Agreement
CWC	Chemical Weapons Convention
DAG	Directed Acyclic Graph
DAO	Decentralized autonomous organization
DGR	Deep Geological Repository
DLT	Distributed Ledger Technology
EDI	Electronic Data Interchange
EDIS	Electronic Declaration Information System
EDNA	Electronic Declaration tool for National Authorities
ERP	Enterprise Resource Planning
EU	European Union
EUC	End-User Certificate
EURATOM	European Atomic Energy Community
GDPR	General Data Protection Regulation
GTGA	Government to government assurances
GUI	Graphical User Interface
GUI	Graphical User Interface
IACC	International Anti-Counterfeiting Coalition Inc
IAEA	International Atomic Energy Agency
ICR	Inventory Change Report
ICT	Information and Communication Technology
INFCIRC	Information Circular

IoT	Internet of Things
IP	Intellectual Property
IPFS	InterPlanetary File System
IPPAS	International Physical Protection Advisory Service
ITT	Intangible Transfers of Technology
KMP	Key Measurement Point
KSI	Keyless Signature Infrastructure
LLNL	Lawrence Livermore National Laboratory
MBA	Material Balance Area
MBR	Material Balance Report
NCA	Nuclear Cooperation Agreement
NGO	Non-governmental Organization
NM	Nuclear Material
NNWS	Non-Nuclear Weapons State
NPT	Treaty on the Proliferation of Nuclear Weapons
NSG	Nuclear Suppliers Group
NUMBAT	Nuclear Material Balances and Tracking
NW	Nuclear Weapons
NWS	Nuclear Weapons State
OPCW	Organisation for the Prohibition of Chemical Weapons
PIL	Physical Inventory Listing
PIV	Physical Inventory Verification
PKI	Public Key Infrastructure
PNNL	Pacific Northwest National Laboratory
SAFKA	Finland's national safeguards database
SCM	Supply Chain Management
SIX	Secure Information Exchange
SLAFKA	Shared Ledger SAFKA
SLUMBAT	Shared Ledger NUMBAT
STUK	Finnish Radiation and Nuclear Safety Authority
TPS	Transactions Per Second
UNSC	United Nations Security Council
UNSCR	United Nations Security Council Resolution
UNSW	University of New South Wales
URL	Uniform Resource Locator
WEF	World Economic Forum
WMD	Weapons of Mass Destruction
WTO	World Trade Organization

List of Figures

List of Tables

Blockchain for International Security an Introduction

Cindy Vestergaard

Abstract International security sits at the point where civilian and military technologies meet—when an innovation yields both benefits for humanity but also the ferocity of modern warfare. The pace of today's innovation is disrupting all sectors, creating more urgency for practitioners and students of international security and emerging technology to interact—not only on the potential for advances to be misused but also how they can be used to strengthen international security. As such, effective implementation of treaties and controls need to strike a balance in allowing the free flow of trade with nonproliferation objectives while keeping pace with scientific and technological innovations that have the potential to disrupt both. Distributed ledger technology (DLT) is one emerging technology that offers solutions for creating greater efficiencies in tracking nuclear, biological, chemical and dual-use materials in line with national and international reporting obligations.

1 Introduction

Inventions that influence international security sit at the intersection of the wheel and fire element of technology: the point where civilian and military meet—when an innovation yields both benefits for humanity but also the ferocity of modern warfare. For almost three centuries, industrial revolutions have bred discoveries and innovations that have led to the doubling of living standards every fifty years [1]. Warfare has kept pace, adopting (and sometimes leading) scientific advances that led to the development of a category of weapons so devastating they could destroy civilization, leaving future wars to be "fought with sticks and stones" [2]. Today's digital world and breakthrough innovations seems to be moving at a more rapid pace, propelling us into the Fourth Industrial Revolution "at an exponential rather than a linear pace" [3]. The pace is disrupting all sectors, whether travel, telecommunications, transport, trade, finance, or warfare, creating more urgency for practitioners and students of

C. Vestergaard (✉)
The Stimson Center, Washington, DC, USA
e-mail: cvestergaard@stimson.org

© Springer Nature Switzerland AG 2021
C. Vestergaard (ed.), *Blockchain for International Security*,
Advanced Sciences and Technologies for Security Applications,
https://doi.org/10.1007/978-3-030-86240-4_1

international security and emerging technology to interact—not only on the potential for advances to be misused but also how they can be used to strengthen international security.

Advances in twentieth century warfare led to profound effects on and off the battlefield. War had become interdisciplinary and industrialized, involving scientists, engineers, medicine, and manufacturing. Chemical, biological, and nuclear materials were weaponized and formed their own category of "weapons of mass destruction" (WMD). At the same time, advances in chemistry, biology, and physics led to the development of medical, agricultural, industrial, and energy processes that fundamentally benefited human life. Fritz Haber, an early twentieth century German chemist, exemplifies this duality as he is known as both the father of chemical warfare for his role in the development and use of chlorine and other poisonous gases in the trenches of World War I, and as the co-father of the Born-Haber cycle, the first process to provide an industrial solution for large-scale synthesis of fertilizers. For the former he was called a murderer [4]; for the latter he was awarded the Nobel Prize in Chemistry in 1918. In total, poisonous warfare developed by Fritz and others resulted in over 90,000 fatalities and 1.3 m casualties during World War I [5]. At the same time, within the next century, an estimated two thirds of annual global food production would come to rely on nitrogen from the Born-Haber process to feed the global population [6].

The next weapon of mass destruction was introduced in 1945 when the US detonated two nuclear weapons over Japan: the first was a uranium-gun type fission bomb detonated over Hiroshima on August 6, 1945, and the second was a plutonium implosion-type bomb over Nagasaki three days later. Estimates of civilian and military killed in total range from 110,000 to a high of 210,000 [7]. While nuclear weapons would not be used again in conflict, more than 2,000 nuclear tests were carried out from 1945 until 1996 when the Comprehensive Test Ban Treaty opened for signature [8]. In the meantime, chemical weapons would become the most used type of WMD in conflict with chemical attacks continuing today in Syria [9].

The totality of twentieth century warfare led to negotiations of treaties attempting to limit (and hopes to eventually eliminate) weapons of mass destruction (WMD). These treaties take shape in multilateral, bilateral, and national rules and regulations that form a complex, layered web of governance over chemical, biological and nuclear materials, and activities. It is a system that engenders caution given the disruptive nature of WMD warfare. It has proven to be a resilient system in part due to this caution, but it is not fool-proof, especially as more technologies are invented and adapted with little thought about how they may affect—or worse, circumvent—these diplomatic milestones. As observed in a 1971 UN report: "each new step in arms development usually leads to a more dangerous stage of uncertainty and weakening of security" [10]. As a result, the culture of international security lies in contrast to the famous Silicon Valley motto of "move fast and break things," now more broadly associated with today's culture of innovation [11].

Then, the year 2020 brought on an unprecedented level of change, one that could fundamentally shift the way we interact with technologies and each other. The COVID-19 pandemic and subsequent health restrictions requiring physical distancing measures led to teleworking on a large scale, demonstrating the resiliency of the internet and information and communication technology (ICT). It is estimated that nearly 40% of the European Union (EU) [12, 13] and close to 62% of Americans were teleworking early in the pandemic [14] with figures in the United States suggesting one in four were teleworking almost a year later [15]. Teleworking is testing traditional perimeter-centric interpretations of security such as secure rooms and buildings which provide defenses and air gaps to guard sensitive information but are impractical if employees cannot access them. Moreover, analogue systems create barriers to teleworking as in Japan where 31% of companies in one poll were unable to telework given paperwork and internal processes had not yet been digitized [16]. COVID-19 restrictions are therefore creating reliance on unattended and "no touch" systems to communicate and securely share information across networks.

Emerging technologies such as artificial intelligence and blockchain technologies can enhance the integrity of data while bridging secure rooms with secure networks while advances in robotics and the Internet of Things (IoT) can help to maintain a continuity of knowledge over unattended systems. Blockchain technology, a subset of distributed ledger technology (DLT), is the focus of this book as it has been increasingly adopted by industries to create greater efficiencies and security across business operations, particularly for supply chains. Data on a DLT platform is extremely difficult to manipulate, allowing stakeholders the ability to share information in a trusted environment. This is in turn has led to an increase in research studying the potential for DLT to track nuclear, biological, and chemical materials in line with national and international reporting obligations. The authors in this book provide an overview of the research done to date on DLT and international security and identify ways in which research can be carried forward to further develop and test the potential for DLT to strengthen international security.

Chapter 2 "Distributed Ledger Technology: Beyond the Hype" by Cindy Vestergaard, Haimanot Anbesaw Bobosha, and Karolin Langfeldt introduces the main technical attributes and functions of DLT and how different types of DLT platforms are used to solve different challenges. It underscores that the technology is still very much in the R&D phase but is rapidly evolving as it is being tested and used for a variety of solutions. It discusses two global supply chain use cases to highlight how different DLT platforms are being commercially used to build trust, data consistency, and persistence through the chain of custody for materials as they transform along the supply chain from source to end-use. Although these use cases are not specific to international security, they are used to manage risks that are like those related to treaties governing the non-proliferation of chemical, biological, and nuclear materials such as provenance of trade and movement of materials and creating greater efficiencies and security in records management and data sharing.

The chapters by Sarah Frazar (chapter 3 on "Blockchain Applications for Nuclear Safeguards") and Dr. Edward Obbard, Edward Yu, and Guntur Dharma Putra (chapter 4 on "Blockchain Tools for Nuclear Safeguards") focus on nuclear safeguards and DLT. Frazar introduces the evolution of the nuclear safeguards system and the core functions and technical objectives of the International Atomic Energy

Agency (IAEA). She discusses the benefits, drawbacks, and international perspectives of deploying DLT for safeguards and presents areas where the technology could be deployed. She notes that, based on research to date, DLT does not solve specific safeguards challenges per se given the safeguards system generally functions well; but that it adds an overall improvement in the level of security, efficiency, transparency, and trust of nuclear safeguards information management. Obbard, Yu, and Putra present two prototypes, SLUMBAT and SLAFKA—the world's first small-scale demonstrations of DLT for nuclear safeguards information management. The chapter compares the development process and design requirements for each and discusses their impact in terms of nuclear safeguards. Both demonstrate how DLT can encode legislation and streamline reporting between stakeholders in complex regulatory ecosystems. SLAFKA, for example, demonstrates how data entered in a DLT system by a nuclear operator can be made available almost simultaneously to three different regulators, with potential for different levels of oversight by each one.

Maria Lovely Umayam discusses the role of nuclear security within the larger nuclear enterprise in chapter 5 on "Possibilities of Blockchain Technology for Nuclear Security ." She outlines the key players responsible for creating and maintaining nuclear security regimes; the challenges that influence the current security landscape and engender distrust among these stakeholders; and what a DLT platform could possibly provide to enhance existing nuclear security approaches. She notes that: the notion of trust in the context of security (especially cyber security) is complicated, given that the standard approach is to "trust nothing and verify everything."

The chapters "Blockchain for Global Trade in Dual-Use Chemicals" and "Blockchain Applications for Export Control Compliance and Global Supply Chain Integrity" move beyond the nuclear sector to focus on trade of materials and technology. Dr. Richard Cupitt (chapter 6 on "Blockchain for Global Trade in Dual-Use Chemicals") assesses the potential for how and where DLT may be most effective in preventing the proliferation of chemical weapons. Specifically, Dr. Cupitt identifies how existing DLT platforms may be used as an initial proof of concept for a DLT-based solution for dual-use chemical trade controls by examining the case of end-user certificates. Lastly, Diego Cándano Laris (chapter 7 on "Blockchain Applications for Export Control Compliance and Global Supply Chain Integrity") outlines how DLT can support effective implementation of export controls by ensuring that strategic military and dual-use goods and technologies are not diverted to unauthorized end-users after crossing borders. Cándano focuses on three potential applications in the field of export controls: sensitive data management; detection and prevention of falsified documents and validation of identities; and traceability of sensitive items.

As a whole, the book aims to present research to date and identify areas where it can go in studying the potential of DLT for international security. It is not meant to be exhaustive as it is the first attempt to bridge the disciplines of international security and blockchain technology to discuss applications for nonproliferation and export controls. Hopefully, it inspires other disciplines such as human security and climate change to consider how DLT can be a "technology for good" in strengthening international security.

References

1. Haldane AG (2015) Growing, fast and slow. Speech delivered at University of East Anglia. 17 Feb 2015, p 4. https://www.bankofengland.co.uk/-/media/boe/files/speech/2015/growing-fast-and-slow.pdf?la=en&hash=621B4A687E7BC1FE101859779E1DFFE546A1449F. Accessed 20 April 2021
2. The full quote by Albert Einstein is: I know not with what weapons World War III will be fought, but World War IV will be fought with sticks and stones. See: Albert Einstein Quotes. BrainyQuote.com, Brainy Media Inc, 2021. https://www.brainyquote.com/quotes/albert_einstein_122873. Accessed 18 June 2021
3. Schwab K (2016) The fourth industrial revolution: what it means, how to respond. World Economic Forum. https://www.weforum.org/agenda/2016/01/the-fourth-industrial-revolution-what-it-means-and-how-to-respond/. Accessed 10 April 2021
4. Bowlby C (2011) Fritz Haber: Jewish chemist whose work led to Zyklon B. BBC Radio 4. https://www.bbc.com/news/world-13015210. Accessed 14 February 2021
5. Haber LF (1986) The poisonous cloud: chemical warfare in the first world war. Clarendon Press, Oxford, p 170
6. Smil V (2004) Enriching the earth: Fritz Haber, Carl Bosch, and the transformation of world food production. MIT Press, Cambridge, Massachusetts, p 156
7. Wellerstein A (2020) Counting the dead at Hiroshima and Nagasaki. Bull Atom Sci. https://thebulletin.org/2020/08/counting-the-dead-at-hiroshima-and-nagasaki/. Accessed 10 April 2021
8. CTBTO (2021) Nuclear testing. https://www.ctbto.org/nuclear-testing/history-of-nuclear-testing/world-overview/. Accessed 10 April 2021
9. Lederer EM (2021) Watchdog: Syria has likely used chemical weapons 17 times. https://apnews.com/article/united-nations-middle-east-syria-europe-business-f82ffb6c25fa46583b16fc2c23614153. Accessed 10 June 2022
10. Kaliadan AN (1972) Problems of disarmament research. J Peace Res 9(3):238. See also: Report of the Secretary-General on the study of the economic and social consequences of the arms race and military expenditures (1988) United Nations Publication, A/43/368
11. Facebook's internal motto was "move fast and break things" until 2014 when it was replaced with "move fast with stable infrastructure." See Baer D (2014) Mark Zuckerberg explains why Facebook doesn't 'move fast and break things' anymore. Insider. https://www.businessinsider.com/mark-zuckerberg-on-facebooks-new-motto-2014-5. Accessed 23 April 2021
12. European Commission (2020) Telework in the EU before and after the COVID-19: where we were, where we head to. Science for Policy Briefs. https://ec.europa.eu/jrc/sites/jrcsh/files/jrc120945_policy_brief_-_covid_and_telework_final.pdf. Accessed 12 May 2021
13. International Labour Organization (2020) Teleworking during the COVID-19 pandemic and beyond: a practical guide, p 6. https://www.ilo.org/wcmsp5/groups/public/---ed_protect/---protrav/---travail/documents/publication/wcms_751232.pdf. Accessed 21 May 2021
14. Brenan M (2020) U.S. Workers discovering affinity for remote work. Gallup News. https://news.gallup.com/poll/306695/workers-discovering-affinity-remote-work.aspx. Accessed 15 April 2021
15. U.S. Bureau of Labor Statistics (2021) Workers aged 25–54 more likely to telework due to Covid-19 in February 2021. https://www.bls.gov/opub/ted/2021/workers-ages-25-to-54-more-likely-to-telework-due-to-covid-19-in-february-2021.htm. Accessed 25 May 2021
16. Berg J, Bonnet F, Soares S (2020) Working from home: establishing the worldwide potential. VOX EU. https://voxeu.org/article/working-home-estimating-worldwide-potential

Distributed Ledger Technology: Beyond the Hype

Cindy Vestergaard, Haimanot Anbesaw Bobosha, and Karolin Langfeldt

Abstract This chapter introduces distributed ledger technology (DLT), its main features, functions, and how different types of platforms are used to solve different challenges. The chapter includes two global supply chain use cases to highlight how different DLT platforms are being commercially used to build trust, data consistency and persistence through the chain of custody for materials as they transform along the supply chain from source to end-use end (and beyond to recycling in one case). Although these use cases are not specific to international security, they are used to manage risks that are similar to those related to treaties governing the nonproliferation of chemical, biological, and nuclear materials such as provenance of trade and movement of materials, and creating greater efficiencies and security in records management and data sharing.

1 Introduction

There has been no shortage of hype around "the blockchain." Its publicity has been tied to the rise of cryptocurrencies, from humble beginnings in 2008 in the cryptography community when the idea for Bitcoin was launched to its association a few years later with the illicit trade of drugs on the dark web [1]. The hype reached a frenzy in 2017 as cryptocurrencies rallied, culminating in the absurd as small public companies raced to capitalize by adding blockchain to their name. One, now infamous case, is that of Long Island Iced Tea Corp which announced in December 2017 it was leaving its ready-to-drink tea business to invest in blockchain technology, changed

C. Vestergaard (✉)
The Stimson Center, Washington, DC, USA
e-mail: cvestergaard@stimson.org

H. A. Bobosha
The Henry L. Stimson Center, Washington, DC, USA

K. Langfeldt
Circulor, London, USA

© Springer Nature Switzerland AG 2021
C. Vestergaard (ed.), *Blockchain for International Security*,
Advanced Sciences and Technologies for Security Applications,
https://doi.org/10.1007/978-3-030-86240-4_2

its name to Long Blockchain, and its stock soared by 500% in a day [2]. By January 2018, the U.S. Securities and Exchange Commission was warning public companies against abrupt shifts in names or business strategies to take advantage of crypto and blockchain hype [3]. Even though there are many today who still conflate Bitcoin with blockchain, there is a wider understanding that blockchain is the digital ledger platform underpinning cryptocurrencies which has wider applications than digital currencies. As noted by one FT reporter, "Blockchain is to Bitcoin, what the internet is to email. A big electronic system, on top of which you can build applications. Currency is just one" [4].

Blockchain is a type of distributed ledger technology (DLT). The blockchain is a block series where transactions are grouped and linked together in "blocks," but not all DLT platforms use blocks. The appeal of DLT is rooted in its ability to establish an immutable system of records management with consensus, and without reliance on a centralized system. DLT creates a shared reality among parties in a way that lowers uncertainty and builds confidence by: (1) providing participants access to the same copy of records in a specific instant; (2) transaction history cannot be changed (immutability) and (3) records are permanently persisted in a way that allows provenance and auditing (auditability) [5]. Major players in the finance, health, and logistics sectors have been testing the technology to understand its potential and many are employing DLT in their global operations.

This chapter will introduce concepts and characteristics of DLT platforms and how its development has propelled use cases for permissioned platforms across enterprises globally. It then describes how DLT works, its main features, and benefits and concludes by providing examples of how the technology is used at the government and industry level.

2   What is Distributed Ledger Technology?

DLT is a set of technologies that enable a consistent representation of data across multiple nodes without a central authority. DLT enables a distributed record or "ledger" in which transactions are stored in a permanent, immutable way with cryptographic techniques, ensuring consistency, provenance, and auditability across the entire ecosystem. Transactions can be easily audited as they are time-stamped and "hashed," essentially a digital fingerprint that interlinks transactions as they are appended to the ledger.

Essentially, DLT is a database that:

> (i) enables a network of independent participants to establish a consensus around (ii) the authoritative ordering of cryptographically validated ("signed") transactions. These records are made (iii) persistent by replicating the data across multiple nodes, and (iv) tamper evident by linking them by cryptographic hashes. (v) The shared result of the reconciliation/consensus process—the "ledger"—serves as the authoritative version for these records [6].

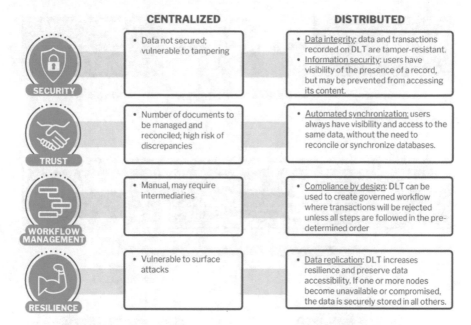

Fig. 1 Centralized ledger versus a distributed ledger [7]

A distributed ledger is decentralized, removing the need for a central authority to process, verify or authenticate transactions. Centralized ledgers on the other hand have one central authority. The difference between the two types of ledgers is described in Fig. 1.

3 Features of Distributed Leger Technology

The main features of DLT include hashing, immutability, peer to peer protocols, and consensus.

Hashing

The hashing algorithm was invented in the 1940s by Hans Peter Luhn, who created a machine and schemes for parsing information that were designed to work for words and sentences [8]. Today, hashing forms the basis of data authentication and security [9]. Hashing is a one-way function that can be applied to any string of input characters to generate a specific fixed-length output—whether numbers, text, whole documents, large files like videos, or even an entire operating system [10]. Its security value is its unidirectional process whereby anyone can confirm content hashes to a certain value, but it is impossible to derive the original content from the hash. Figure 2 outlines the hashing function.

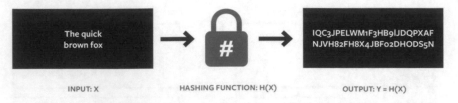

Fig. 2 Hashing [7]

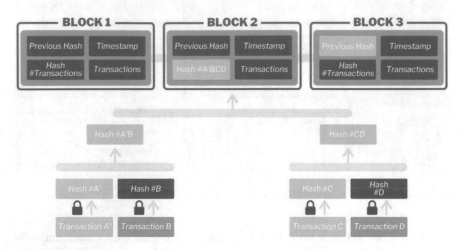

Fig. 3 Immutability [7]

Immutability

Each block stores the hash of its predecessor, serving as a type of DNA strand that connects each transaction and block on the blockchain. Hashing, coupled with the append only structure of DLT, provides for immutability in which a transaction cannot be changed after it is recorded on the ledger as depicted in Fig. 3. If Transaction A was modified to Transaction A', then Block 2 would be stored as #A'BCD which would no longer correspond to the previous hash in Block 3.

Peer-to-Peer (P2P)

In its simplest form, a peer-to-peer network is created when two or more devices are connected and share resources without going through a separate server. The concept of peer-to-peer networking has been around since 1969, but the first dial-up P2P network, Usenet, was created in 1980 as a worldwide internet discussion system [10]. DLT uses P2P to avoid the prevalent server—client structure by allowing network participants to exchange data that is verified and stored by the network. DLT's P2P architecture allows all transactions to be transferred to all network participant nodes, where each keeps a complete copy of the ledger and compares it to the other nodes to ensure that the transaction is accurate [11]. P2P networking is

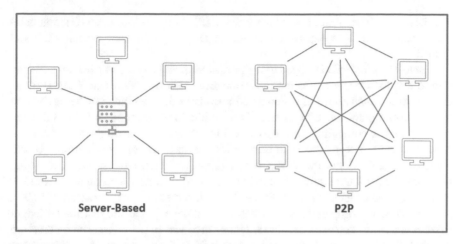

Fig. 4 Server-based network versus P2P network [7]

a distributed architecture as opposed to the traditional server-based architecture as depicted in Fig. 4.

Consensus

Consensus protocols are the rules and methods by which transaction validation is settled on by nodes in a distributed ledger. Consensus is the trust mechanism for authentication and access controls. Early protocols developed in the 1980s and 1990s relied heavily on a cryptographic primitive known as 'Chaumian Blinding' which is the method of performing a transaction without having to know who is present from both sides of the transaction, including the time and content. Chaumian Blinding was invented by David Lee Chaum and published in the paper "Blind Signatures for Untraceable Payments" in 1982 [12].

Early attempts at developing digital currencies led to advances in consensus where algorithms developed to limit denial of service attacks (such as that used by Hashcash in 1987) [13] or to use computing power to solve cryptographic puzzles which were time stamped and added to the next puzzle to form a chain of records as with Bit gold which was launched in 1998 [14]. Its founder Nick Szabo also proposed "a solution to secure namespaces and similar problems as well as the problem of securely recording agreements on traditional property rights" and "how new developments in replicated database technology allows for the secure management and transfer of ownership for a wide range of property" [15]. Wei Dai also published a paper titled "b-money, an anonymous distributed electronic cash system" in 1998, which identified the core concepts later adopted by Bitcoin and other cryptocurrencies, such as solving computational puzzles and decentralized consensus [16], but it was limited in explaining how decentralized consensus could be implemented [17]. With Bitcoin, financial incentives were added for maintaining the connected copies of the ledger which became the foundation for the proof of work consensus [18].

These advances in turn helped to evolve DLT platforms into three different categories based on how consensus is organized: open/permissionless, permissioned, and hybrid.

Open DLT platforms are open to the public, allowing anyone to participate. Many public cryptocurrency platforms including Bitcoin use a "Proof of Work (PoW)" consensus as noted above in which a node validates the next block by being the first to solve a computer-intensive puzzle. The likelihood of a new block being validated depends on the computing power assigned to the task. The node (miner) will get a certain amount of crypto assets or transaction fees as a reward for validating a block. Because the miners get incentives, they support and secure the network, allowing it to become profitable rather than attacking it and making it unprofitable. Another consensus mechanism, "Proof of Stake (PoS)" is a method where, instead of PoW's energy intensive computations, an established stake in a specific distributed ledger system is used to achieve consensus. Nodes involved in the consensus method are compensated by collecting transaction fees included in each block that they are the first to successfully validate.

Permissioned DLT platforms restrict access to a specific set of participants. Permissioned, enterprise platforms are rapidly advancing as more enterprises/consortiums are developing them to meet specific scalability and governance requirements within different business models and their global operations [24]. For example, Hyperledger Fabric uses "endorsement policies" in which a set of policy requirements guide the acceptance of such transactions by network users. Indeed, Hyperledger Fabric [19] is one of the most well-known and widely used system for deploying and operating permissioned platforms. Launched in 2015, Hyperledger was put under the Linux Foundation when many organizations wanted to achieve more by working together to create open-source frameworks, tools, and libraries for enterprise blockchain solutions [20]. It provides an option for allowing only approved parties to replicate data on the platform, providing the benefits of DLT for decentralized consensus, immutability, data integrity and authentication [21]. Circulor, one of the use cases discussed in the case study section below, uses Hyperledger Fabric.

Consensus mechanisms in permissioned platforms are faster and more energy efficient than for open platforms. Since security is managed by access control, permissioned ledgers need less processing resources to maintain consistency, and the benefits of speed and reliability are likely to be maintained. For example, Bitcoin can process a transaction at a rate of 5 to a maximum of seven tps (transactions per second). If the transaction is complex, with five inputs, the rate is two tps, but theoretically ten tps, and the transaction must wait for a new block to be processed, which could take up to ten minutes. A permissioned DLT framework. such as the Hyperledger Fabric can process 20,000 transactions per second [22] while Guardtime's KSI can process billions per second [23]. However, new permissionless blockchain platforms such as Avalanche and Algorand, both for decentralized finance, are on the rise, with tps exceeding 1000. Avalanche is a new blockchain network developed by Ava labs that employs a proof of stake consensus mechanism to achieve high throughput, which is expected to exceed 4500 tps [24]. On the other hand, according to company website, Algorand is "the world's first pure proof-of-stake foundational blockchain designed for the future of finance," [25] and it aims to increase throughput to 46,000 tps from 10,000 tps [26].

Guardtime's KSI is the platform underlying Estonia's e-government system. Guardtime was founded in 2007, the same year that cyber-attacks on Estonia took down government communications, banking services and media outlets. In 2008, Guardtime was contracted for certifying the integrity of the digital registries and repositories and [27] by 2012, Estonia became the first nation to adopt DLT as a layer within its government structures.

Open DLT platforms and permissioned platforms both use distributed data structures and consensus to validate transactions but with different assumptions to solve different sets of problems. The Bitcoin blockchain for example solves the issue of double spending while Guardtime focuses on governance, applying DLT at an operational level beyond cryptocurrency.

Hybrid distributed ledger platforms combine the privacy advantages of a permissioned distributed ledger system with the protection and accountability advantages of permissionless distributed ledger systems. This gives organizations flexibility in deciding what information they want to make public and what information they want to keep private [28]. Governments, for example, can use hybrid DLT in a voting system [29] where they can verify a voter or auditor prior to participation while also making the voting system transparent and publicly auditable. For example, Voatz was used in West Virginia during the 2018 U.S. midterm elections, [30] by Denver County during the 2019 US Municipal Election, and by Utah County during the 2020 US Presidential Election [31].

Figure 5 outlines the main differences between open and permissioned DLT platforms.

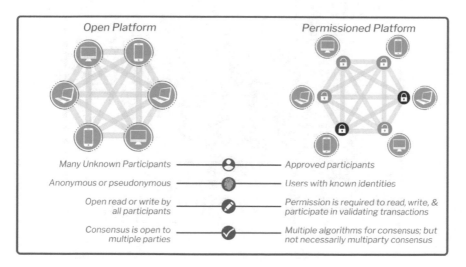

Fig. 5 Public open platform versus private permissioned platform [7]

4 What is in a Block?

A block is composed of a block header and records of transactions. The block header contains block number, current timestamp that captures the date and time to ensure a record of a chronological sequence, the hash of a previous block to link the blocks together and the hash of what is called the "Merkel Root" which allows easy composition and verification of larger data sets of transactions.

In public DLT platforms, a block header includes the "nonce," a random sequence of numbers that the miners must find to validate the blocks. It refers to the first number a blockchain miner needs to discover and include in a block [32]. Miners stop calculating the nonce once they find one that works, allowing them to submit their block for approval by the rest of the nodes. It is important to note that a nonce is difficult to calculate which in turn makes it difficult to work out a block with different data and ruin consensus. It is also considered a way to cut out the less talented miners from the system [33]. To provide an additional level of security, permissioned DLT platform nodes include an access-control layer. In addition to the other components of a block, digital signatures are an important component used to prove transaction ownership.

The first block in any blockchain-based protocol is called the genesis block. Every block stores a reference to the previous block other than the genesis block; the technology uses cryptographic signatures (hashes) to facilitate this. Figure 6 outlines the contents of a block.

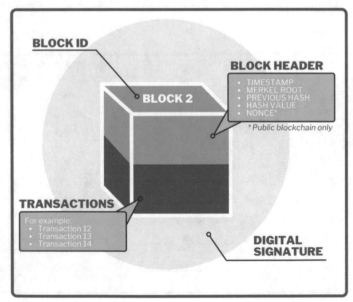

Components of a Block

Fig. 6 What is in a block [7]

5 How DLT Records Transactions

The steps involved in transactions in a permissioned DLT are depicted in Fig. 7 [34].

Step 1:

A DLT transaction requires a digital asset, or a document. The transaction is requested by a participant to upload a document to the platform.

When a transaction is submitted, a key pair is generated by the requester, including a public key that is made available to other network participants. A key-pair is generated only once, not every time a transaction is submitted. The requester then hashes the data to be sent, converts it into a new digital string of predefined and fixed hash length. The hash is signed with the private key using public–private key cryptography. The requester then transmits the digital signature to participants in the peer-to-peer network with the plaintext data.

Step 2:

Transaction is broadcasted to peer-to-peer network participants—the receivers, often called nodes—and added to an unvalidated transaction pool.

Step 3:

Receivers—in the case of permissioned blockchains, authorized nodes—validate the transaction using the requester's public key to decrypt the transaction. A successful decryption confirms that the transaction originates from the claimed sender. The

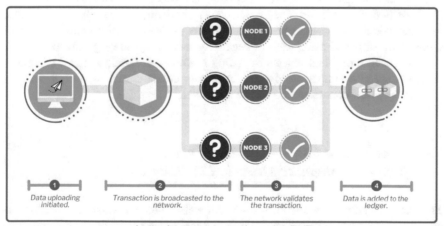

A step by step transaction using DLT

Fig. 7 Transaction in a permissioned DLT platform [7]

network participants can then verify the integrity of data by comparing the decrypted hash value sent by the sender with the hash value that was computed when applying the same hash algorithm on the plain data transmitted by the sender.

Validated transactions are combined with other transactions to create a block that is then validated based on the consensus protocol of the platform. If validated, the new block is linked to the chain as the "true state of the ledger."

Step 4:

Once the transaction has been validated, it is time-stamped and linked to the preceding blocks/transactions with a "hash pointer"—a hash of the previous block/transaction—thereby forming a linear chronological chain of blocks/transactions.

The transaction is then confirmed, and the block/transaction cannot be altered or removed—thus, the block/transaction is immutable. Each time a block/transaction is added to the chain, the digital ledger is updated on all the participating nodes.

6 Operationalizing DLT

The following case studies provide examples of various DLT platforms currently being used. The first is the case of Circulor, a software company that has developed a solution for tracking raw materials and proving their provenance [35]. Second, the AURA platform, the world's first global blockchain designed to assist consumers in tracing the provenance and authenticity of luxury goods [36]. The two use cases are from vastly different fields. They do, however, share one feature: they both involve multiple stakeholders dealing with confidential or proprietary information on a global scale. They also address questions regarding various types of platforms: how to connect specific physical objects or analog resources to specific digital content or digital twins in a tamper-proof manner; how to create clarity to opaque areas of activity; and how counterfeiting can be mitigated.

6.1 Circulor and Volvo—Tracking Cobalt from the Congolese Mines to Car Batteries

The Cobalt Supply Chain involves a complex web of highly diverse actors upstream, which is further complicated by difficult political conditions, corruption, and other general conditions, especially for foreign companies. The lack of transparency begins in the mines, where child labor and exploitation are common issues. One third of the cobalt mined in the Democratic Republic of Congo (DRC) is extracted by hand by independent miners, which represents around 20% of the global supply [37]. Cobalt is then sold to traders and large mining companies, making it difficult to know whether it comes from sustainable and ethical sources. Once cobalt leaves the mines, it passes through a number of actors and intermediaries that often cover all five continents [38]. These actors include miners, smelters, refiners, precursor and cathode producers, and battery manufacturers. As is often the case with traditional supply chains, intermediaries usually know only the immediate supplier or customer in the chain. Mistrust and competition define the relationship between the parties concerned.

Circulor pioneered its technology platform for tracking the cobalt supply chain in 2017 by combining DLT and other technologies to create an immutable chain of custody record for materials as they transform during their journey from source to end-use in a car. DLT was chosen in addition to database technology for three main reasons. Firstly (and primarily) for its immutability, given that it involves multiple parties creating a digital chain of custody. Secondly, because the chain of custody must persist through the entire circular economy of the battery (the battery passport): through in-life uses and then on to recycling. Thirdly, because the solution needs to be able to interoperate and connect with other systems and networks.

At each point of the supply chain, a different data handling system, sometimes even manual paperwork, is in place, making collaboration difficult and transparency almost impossible. Moreover, the raw materials, by their nature, are difficult to reliably tag—the material transforms on its journey from source to end-use; thus, after each transformation, a new identity must be added which inherits the origin of the material and destroys the old identity. Cobalt ore, for example, is transformed into cobalt hydroxide and is further combined with nickel and manganese at different ratios depending on the chemistry to form the precursor. The precursor is then processed into cathode and produced into cells that are then inserted into batteries or electric vehicles. The end product bears no resemblance to the original mined material.

Circulor pioneered its technology platform for tracking the cobalt supply chain in 2017 by combining DLT and other technologies to create an immutable chain of custody record for materials as they transform during their journey from source to end-use in a car. The system provides materials with a unique identity and then tracks their flow as it changes through processing and manufacturing. The system uses IoT and tags to generate digital twins, as well as machine learning to detect anomalies and combat fraud, as well as identify supply chain weaknesses to target due diligence and compliance activities. Circulor currently uses AI for image analysis to ensure security by detecting and recognizing objects. In mid-February 2020, the Swedish car manufacturer Volvo Cars released its first fully electric vehicle, the XC40 Recharge, whose cobalt supply chain is fully traceable on the Circulor platform [39].

Given that some of the data can be sensitive, Circulor uses a private permissioned blockchain—Hyperledger Fabric—to preserve the privacy of participants as well as their data. Furthermore, Oracle Cloud Services provides enterprise-level security and in-depth authentication capabilities and is used to manage access rights and ensure security, reliability, and availability of data. Circulor's customers and participating organizations determine the access rights of users within their organization and private channels on the blockchain ensure that sensitive data can be shared within an organization, without providing visibility to the broader supply chain network [40].

There are several options to upload data to the blockchain [40]:

1. The data can be provided to the blockchain via system integration using RESTful Web Service Application Programming Interface (API) with security and authentication protocols. RESTful APIs are available as integration points from any existing IT system to the Circulor system to securely provide digital chain of custody information that is updated on the blockchain—serving as an immutable record of traceability and provenance. Data transmission using RESTful APIs is secured via state-of-the-art privacy protocols including the use of Secure Sockets Layer (SSL) encryption providing an end-to-end encrypted link to the customer and the Circulor system, in addition to OAuth 2.0 authentication. These measures ensure that data is protected and only visible to authorised users.
2. Via the desktop application, data can be manually entered or uploaded.
3. The mobile application can be used to upload data via scans and manual entry to ensure an inclusive low barrier to entry for all participants.

Circulor uses other technology to prove that the data entered into the system is correct, such as AI, GPS fencing, and facial recognition, because validation has to happen before the data enters the system. Material verification begins at source throughout the supply chain. Circulor uses DLT in conjunction with mine site inspections, GPS tracking, entry and exit scanning, verified logistics providers, facial recognition, Id checks and time tracking, which contribute to the traceability of materials from the mine to the car factory [40]. Registered users in the field are checked using facial recognition via an app. The material is registered in the system with checks on the location of origin and checks to counter the risk that the material is imported from other locations. Each material badge is tagged with a tamper-proof QR-code generated by the Circulor system. The QR code specifies the time, location, weight, person delivering the badge and the person receiving the badge. The number of QR codes issued on that day is registered. In addition, the app that scans the QR code can only be used in a predefined radius. Each anomaly is automatically flagged in the system.

The material will be transported through purchase or sorting centers to raw refining smelters, where the material (cobalt hydroxide) is processed. This product is then shipped, usually to China, for the next steps in refining. The refined material is used to make the cathode for the cells of the battery. In the mid-stream of this supply chain, data is collected directly from the production control and management systems used at each stage via the API.

In addition, Circulor uses a number of verification tests, such as elapsed time or mass balance, to check that there are no anomalies and that the chain of retention of the material is maintained to ensure that the input components of each process can be reliably linked to the output. This process takes place at every step of the battery that is eventually installed in a car. The solution needed to extend Volvo Cars entire battery supply chain for electric vehicles (EV) to ensure full traceability of cobalt from source to the EV itself.

The aim was to manage the risk and demonstrate with as much certainty as possible that material that was produced responsibly throughout the supply chain at every stage. Following the success of this work, Volvo Cars is now extending the use of the platform to other mining materials.

6.2 AURA—A Consortium Model Powered by Ethereum Quorum

According to official figures, counterfeit products cost the European Union's apparel, footwear, and accessories industry approximately €26.3 billion (approximately US$27.7 billion) each year [41]. According to the OECD and the EU's Intellectual Property Office, global imports of counterfeit and pirated goods are worth nearly half a trillion dollars per year, or about 2.5% of global imports [42]. In the United States and Europe, counterfeiting/intellectual property (IP) theft are federal and state crimes "that involve the production and distribution of goods in the name of another person without their permission" [43]. Counterfeit goods are typically made from lower-quality components sold at a low-cost to imitate well-known and trusted brands [43].

DLT is a better solution than traditional databases in this case because a traditional database is centrally managed by a trusted administrator, whereas blockchain is jointly owned by a consortium. Furthermore, the luxury goods industry requires a data store that can be written to and accessed by multiple parties such as luxury brand designers, manufactures and distributers, and DLT is a more cost-effective and trustworthy solution than a traditional database. DLT also outperforms traditional databases in terms of historical tracking for auditability and transparency.

Many specialized actors are involved in the luxury goods industry, including designers, producers of raw materials, manufacturers, and distributors. LVMH Moët Hennessy Louis Vuitton commonly known as LVMH, is a French multinational corporation and conglomerate specializing in luxury goods, headquartered in Paris, France [44]. LVMH collaborated with Microsoft and blockchain software company ConsenSys to develop the AURA platform, a hybrid DLT system aimed at serving the entire luxury industry with product tracking and tracing services based on Ethereum and utilizing Microsoft Azure [45]. With AURA, consumers can track the lifecycle of their products, from design and raw materials to manufacturing, and distribution. The platform is built on Traceability Smart Contracts (ERC 721 non-fungible token standards [46]) and the AURA blockchain infrastructure, a permissioned consortium network based on Quorum to ensure no information in leaked between brands or their customers [47].

The platform is hybrid, meaning some procedures and information are kept private while others are made public. The most significant advantage of using a hybrid platform is having more control over the network. AURA runs behind the brands using it. During production, each product is irreproducible and contains unique information, which is recorded on the shared ledger. At the time of purchase, a consumer can use the brand's application to receive the AURA certificate containing all product information. It could, for example, identify an individual handbag and trace its entire lifecycle from an alligator farm to the store where it was first sold, and then multiple chains of owners who have owned and sold it [48].

The AURA platform is an example of how DLT provides transparency and a single source of truth for the consumer: it ensures the authenticity of the product, provides details on product origin and components (including ethical and environmental information), instructions for product care, and the after-sales and warranty services that are available.

7 Conclusion

Advances in distributed ledger technology over the past ten years have propelled the technology forward both in public and permissioned applications. Permissioned systems have allowed DLT to be adopted in global operations, streamlining, and securing records management across consortiums while tracking supply chains and their materials. These enterprise solutions have moved DLT beyond the hype, demonstrating its ability to provide wide ranging benefits which in turn may benefit applications for international security.

Although the use cases in this chapter are not specific to international security, they are used to manage risks to commercial supply chains that are similar to challenges faced in the implementation of non-proliferation treaties governing nuclear, chemical, and biological materials and technology where immutability, trust, and a single source of truth would benefit industry and regulators.

References

1. Silk Road (2011–2013) was a digital marketplace mostly for trading illegal drugs on the dark web which used payments in bitcoin. For a good read on Silk Road's rise and fall see: Bearman J (2015) Silk road: the untold story, Wired. https://www.wired.com/2015/05/silk-road-untold-story/. Accessed 8 Feb 2021
2. Kosoff M (2017) Iced tea company changes name to long blockchain, stock immediately skyrockets. https://www.vanityfair.com/news/2017/12/iced-tea-company-changes-name-to-long-blockchain-stock-immediately-skyrockets. Accessed 8 Feb 2021
3. Tepper F (2018) SEC warns against public companies adding blockchain to their name. https://techcrunch.com/2018/01/25/sec-warns-against-public-companies-adding-blockchain-to-their-name/. Accessed 8 Feb 2021
4. Marr B (2018) A very brief history of blockchain technology everyone should read. https://www.forbes.com/sites/bernardmarr/2018/02/16/a-very-brief-history-of-blockchain-technology-everyone-should-read/?sh=1cb5419d7bc4. Accessed 10 Feb 2021
5. Warburg B (2016), How the blockchain will radically transform the economy, TED Talk. https://www.ted.com/talks/bettina_warburg_how_the_blockchain_will_radically_transform_the_economy. Accessed 10 Feb 2021

6. Rauchs M et al (2018) Distributed ledger technology systems. Cambridge Center for Alternative Finance. https://www.jbs.cam.ac.uk/wp-content/uploads/2020/08/2018-10-26-conceptualising-dlt-systems.pdf. Accessed 27 Apr 2021
7. Persi Paoli G, Vestergaard C (2021) Exploring distributed ledger technology for arms control and non-proliferation: a primer. UNIDIR. https://www.unidir.org/publication/exploring-distributed-ledger-technology-arms-control-and-non-proliferation-primer. Accessed 10 Sept 2021
8. Stevens H (2018) Hans Peter Luhn and the birth of the hashing algorithm. https://spectrum.ieee.org/tech-history/silicon-revolution/hans-peter-luhn-and-the-birth-of-the-hashing-algorithm. Accessed 28 Apr 2021
9. Vestergaard C et al (2020) SLAFKA—demonstrating the potential for distributed ledger technology for nuclear safeguards information management. https://www.stimson.org/2020/slafka/. Accessed 20 Feb 2021
10. Touron M (2019) What you should know about the history of P2P https://manfred.life/history-p2p. Accessed 28 Apr 2021
11. Sharma T.K (2020) Blockchain & role of P2P Network. https://www.blockchain-council.org/blockchain/blockchain-role-of-p2p-network/. Accessed 20 Apr 2021
12. Chaum D (1982) Blind signature for untraceable payments. http://www.hit.bme.hu/~buttyan/courses/BMEVIHIM219/2009/Chaum.BlindSigForPayment.1982.PDF. Accessed 20 Apr 2021
13. Back A (2002) Hashcash—a denial of service counter-measure. http://www.hashcash.org/papers/hashcash.pdf. Accessed 20 Apr 2021
14. Szabo N (2008), Unenumerated—an unending variety of topics, bit gold. https://unenumerated.blogspot.com/2005/12/bit-gold.html. Accessed½ 25 Apr 2021
15. Szabo Nick (1998) Secure property titles with owner authority. https://nakamotoinstitute.org/secure-property-titles/. Accessed 25 Apr 2021
16. Dai W (1998) B-money. http://www.weidai.com/bmoney.txt. Accessed 25 Apr 2021
17. Buterin V (2013) Ethereum whitepaper: a next generation smart contract and decentralized application platform. https://ethereum.org/en/whitepaper/. Accessed 30 Apr 2021
18. Narayanan, A et al (2016) Bitcoin and cryptocurrency technologies. https://www.lopp.net/pdf/princeton_bitcoin_book.pdf. Accessed 30 Apr 2021
19. Hyperledger (2021) Advancing business blockchain adoption through global open-source collaboration. https://www.hyperledger.org. Accessed 25 Apr 2021
20. Hyperledger (2018) An introduction to Hyperledger, V1.1. https://www.hyperledger.org/wp-content/uploads/2018/08/HL_Whitepaper_IntroductiontoHyperledger.pdf. Accessed 26 Apr 2021
21. Androulaki E et al (2018) Hyperledger fabric: a distributed operating system for permissioned blockchains. https://arxiv.org/pdf/1801.10228.pdf. Accessed 8 Feb 2021
22. Gorenflo C et al (2019) FastFabric: scaling Hyperledger Fabric to 20,000 transactions per second. https://arxiv.org/pdf/1901.00910.pdf. Accessed 8 Feb 2021
23. Guardtime (2017) Federal keyless signature Infrastructure (KSI) technology: an introduction to KSI Blockchain technology and its benefits, http://blockchain.machetemag.com/wp-content/uploads/2017/11/Guardtime_WhitePaper_KSI.pdf. Accessed 7 Feb 2021, p 8
24. Avalanche (2021) Why Avalanche? https://www.avalabs.org/why-avalanche. Accessed 11 May 2021
25. Algorand. https://www.algorand.com/. Accessed 20 Apr 2021
26. Algorand (2021) What to expect in 2021. https://community.algorand.org/blog/algorand-what-to-expect-in-2021/. Accessed 20 May 2021
27. Guardtime (2016) Lifetrack medical systems upgrades its digital radiology platform with Guardtime's KSI blockchain technology. https://guardtime.com/blog/lifetrack-medical-systems-upgrades-its-digital-radiology-platform-with-guardtime-s-ksi-blockchain-te. Accessed 25 Apr 2021
28. International Telecommunications Unit (2019) ITU-T focus group on application of distributed ledger technology (FG DLT): technical report FG DLT D1.2, p 2. https://www.itu.int/en/ITU-T/focusgroups/dlt/Documents/d12.pdf. Accessed 21 May 2021

29. Geronion D (2021) Hybrid blockchain: the best of both worlds https://101blockchains.com/hybrid-blockchain/. Accessed 21 May 2021
30. Voatz (2021) Secure, Accessible voting at your fingertips. https://voatz.com/. Accessed 21 Mar 2021
31. Specter A et al (2020) The ballot is busted before the blockchain: a security analysis of Voatz, the first internet voting application used in U.S. federal elections. https://internetpolicy.mit.edu/wp-content/uploads/2020/02/SecurityAnalysisOfVoatz_Public.pdf. Accessed 21 May 2021
32. Antonopolous A (2014) Mastering bitcoin. O'Reilly, Sebastol. https://www.oreilly.com/library/view/mastering-bitcoin/9781491902639/ch08.html. Accessed 15 Feb 2021
33. Frankenfield J (2021) Nonce. https://www.investopedia.com/terms/n/nonce.asp. Accessed 15 Feb 2021
34. 101 Blockchains (2020) How blockchain records all the transactions? Fundamentals explained. https://101blockchains.com/blockchain-records-transactions/. Accessed 10 June 2021
35. Circulor (2021) About. https://www.circulor.com/about. Accessed 10 June 2021
36. The AURA blockchain consortium. https://auraluxuryblockchain.com/. Accessed 15 June 2021
37. Walt V (2018) Blood, sweat and batteries. https://fortune.com/longform/blood-sweat-and-batteries/. Accessed 20 Mar 2021 Volvo (2019)
38. Mancini L et al (2020) JRC technical report: responsible and sustainable sourcing of battery raw materials. https://publications.jrc.ec.europa.eu/repository/bitstream/JRC120422/surebatt_report_final_26_06_2020_%281%29.pdf. Accessed 20 Mar 2021
39. Available at Volvo cars to implement blockchain traceability of cobalt used in electric car batteries. https://www.media.volvocars.com/global/en-gb/media/pressreleases/260242/volvo-cars-to-implement-blockchain-traceability-of-cobalt-used-in-electric-car-batteries. Accessed 15 Feb 2021
40. Written communication with Circulor. 10 May 2021
41. EUIPO (2021) The economic cost of IPR infringement in the clothing, footwear and accessories sector. https://euipo.europa.eu/ohimportal/en/web/observatory/ip-infringements_clothing-accessories-footwear. Accessed 17 Apr 2021
42. OECD (2016) Global trade in fake goods worth nearly half a trillion dollars a year—OECD & EUIPO. https://www.oecd.org/industry/global-trade-in-fake-goods-worth-nearly-half-a-trillion-dollars-a-year.htm. Accessed 17 Apr 2021
43. IACC (2021) What is counterfeiting? https://www.iacc.org/resources/about/what-is-counterfeiting. Accessed 26 Mar 2021
44. LVMH (2021). https://www.lvmh.com/. Accessed 26 Mar 2021
45. ConsenSys (2019) LVMH, consensys, and microsoft announce consortium for luxury industry. https://consensys.net/blog/press-release/lvmh-microsoft-consensys-announce-aura-to-power-luxury-industry/. Accessed 27 Mar 2021
46. Ethereum (2021) ERC 721 non-fungible token standard. https://ethereum.org/en/developers/docs/standards/tokens/erc-721/. Accessed 27 May 2021
47. Quorum (2021). https://consensys.net/quorum/. Accessed 27 Mar 2021
48. Allison I (2019) Louis Vuitton owner LVMH is launching a blockchain to track luxury goods. https://tokenlandia.com/news/louis-vuitton-owner-lvmh-is-launching-a-blockchain-to-track-luxury-goods/. Accessed 24 Mar 2021

Blockchain Applications for Nuclear Safeguards

Sarah Frazar

Abstract This chapter discusses the benefits and challenges of using distributed ledger technology (DLT) for international nuclear safeguards purposes. The chapter introduces the international safeguards system and the role of the International Atomic Energy Agency (IAEA). The chapter describes the evolution of the safeguards system, the IAEA's core functions, and the technical objectives it seeks to achieve. The chapter explains the benefits and drawbacks of deploying DLT for safeguards and presents potential use cases where the technology could be deployed. It ends with a description of the international community's current perspectives on deployment.

1 Introduction

Since the creation and use of nuclear weapons (NW) in 1945, the risk of proliferation of equipment, materials, and knowledge related to NW has been nearly universally recognized as presenting a grave threat to international peace. The international community has put in place an elaborate architecture of institutional and technical measures to mitigate this risk. The dynamic nature of the proliferation threat requires a myriad of technical and policy solutions to help monitor changes in nuclear inventories, track movements of nuclear material, and verify the ultimate owner, location, and use of nuclear material. Distributed ledger technology (DLT) is one such technical solution under consideration for a variety of national security-related applications. While this book discusses the benefits and drawbacks of using DLT to help address a

---

Disclaimer: The views expressed in this article do not necessarily represent the views of the Pacific Northwest National Laboratory or the United States.

S. Frazar (✉)
Global Security Technology and Policy Group, Pacific Northwest National Laboratory, Seattle, WA, USA
e-mail: Sarah.frazar@pnnl.gov

© Springer Nature Switzerland AG 2021
C. Vestergaard (ed.), *Blockchain for International Security*,
Advanced Sciences and Technologies for Security Applications,
https://doi.org/10.1007/978-3-030-86240-4_3

variety of international security problems, this chapter focuses on the challenges and opportunities associated with using DLT to benefit the nuclear safeguards system.

The chapter begins with a description of the legal underpinnings that dictate whether and how new technologies are accepted for safeguards use. The chapter describes the political challenges inherent in the safeguards system and discusses how political and legal questions have shaped the community's perceptions of deploying DLT for safeguards use. The chapter ends with a discussion about the different use cases where DLT might be beneficial to safeguards while recognizing the barriers that must be overcome for the technology to be successfully deployed.

2   Overview of International Nuclear Safeguards

Proliferation risks have evolved significantly since NW technology first appeared. Over the years, while a handful of countries developed nuclear capabilities for military purposes, dozens of countries developed and applied nuclear technology for peaceful applications. Today, nuclear material like uranium, plutonium, and thorium can be found in applications such as energy generation, medical and scientific research, radiation shielding, counterweights, industrial applications, and space equipment. In the energy generation field, as of 2019, there were 450 nuclear power reactors operating in 30 countries with another 53 reactors under construction [1]. These facilities and the associated nuclear fuel cycle facilities use, process, and store nuclear material that could be misused to advance a clandestine NW program.

To help mitigate the proliferation risk posed by increasing use of nuclear material for peaceful applications, the International Atomic Energy Agency (IAEA) applies international safeguards, which refers to technical measures applied by the IAEA on nuclear material and facilities. These measures enable the IAEA to verify that States are in compliance with obligations to use nuclear material for peaceful purposes. These obligations are derived from safeguards agreements between the State and the IAEA. Through the 1960s, when the number of nuclear facilities and NM inventories was still relatively limited, safeguards agreements focused on specific facilities and on selected materials [2]. By the late 1960s, as more countries continued to conduct nuclear tests, strengthen their nuclear capabilities, and increase their NM inventories, the international community recognized the need for a comprehensive approach for ensuring the peaceful use of nuclear technology and successfully negotiated the Treaty on the Nonproliferation of Nuclear Weapons (NPT) [3]. Today, the NPT is the cornerstone of a system designed to prevent the spread of nuclear weapons and weapons technology while promoting peaceful uses of nuclear energy.

This system has grown and evolved during the past fifty years around a set of legal agreements that underpin all safeguards verification activities performed by the IAEA.[1] In accordance with the terms and conditions of these agreements, the IAEA

---

[1] The type of safeguards agreement a State signs is determined by its status under the NPT. Non-nuclear weapons state (NNWS) parties to the NPT, or States that did not detonate a nuclear explosive

performs verification activities such as collecting and evaluating safeguards-relevant information, inspecting nuclear installations, verifying States' declarations of nuclear material, and verifying facility declared designs [5]. The IAEA uses a robust process to explore, evaluate and accept the use of new equipment and technologies to carry out these safeguards functions to ensure conformity with the obligations of the safeguards agreement.

Herein lies a significant challenge facing the IAEA when considering cutting-edge technologies such as DLT. The IAEA has a strong interest in introducing new technologies that could improve the efficiency and effectiveness of its safeguards implementation activities, which are performed in a severely constrained budgetary environment [8].[2] Yet, the process of integrating new technologies into the international safeguards system involves a level of complexity not found in national regulatory systems or in commercial industries. Unlike national laws and regulations, which can be developed and updated to reflect a changing environment, the obligations and requirements reflected in the model safeguards agreement [4] were carefully negotiated by the IAEA and the international community and explicitly reiterated in hundreds of safeguards agreements with very minor modifications that are tailored to meet the conditions of each State. The IAEA is unlikely to accept a new technology that would alter, undermine, or impact these carefully negotiated agreements. Moreover, the IAEA is unlikely to renegotiate hundreds of safeguards agreements to accommodate a new technology.

Thus, these legal obligations require thoughtful consideration before introducing new technologies, particularly technologies such as DLT that ostensibly disrupt safeguards verification activities. Specifically, the IAEA considers whether the benefits of introducing the technology will outweigh the potential disruption. Commercial experience using DLT to manage various industry supply chains suggest the benefits of introducing the technology for safeguards use might lead to improvements in operational efficiency, data quality, information security, and in the IAEA's ability to monitor movements of nuclear material within and between States. The challenge facing the IAEA lies in evaluating whether the strict legal framework and political complexities inherent in the safeguards system minimize or preclude any of the benefits that are enjoyed by commercial industries. Such evaluation starts with discussion about the major legal and political questions that arise from technology deployment. Some of these questions are addressed in the following sections.

---

device before January 1, 1967, are required to conclude a Comprehensive Safeguards Agreement (CSA), which places all nuclear material and facilities under safeguards [4]. Nuclear weapons state (NWS) parties to the NPT, or States that had detonated nuclear explosive device before January 1, 1967, may sign a Voluntary Offer Agreement (VOA). Non-NPT signatories may sign an item-specific safeguards agreement [2, 5, 6]. States that have signed a VOA or item-specific safeguards agreement agree to place selected materials and facilities under safeguards. Finally, a State may also choose to sign an additional protocol (AP) to its safeguards agreement which affords the IAEA expanded information about a States' nuclear activities and better tools to detect undeclared activities [6, 7].

[2] Due to a well-established zero or near-zero real growth pressure on the Agency's regular budget, coupled with increasing responsibilities and other budgetary requests, the IAEA remains underfunded to perform its normative functions.

3 Legal and Political Factors Influencing DLT Acceptance for Safeguards Use

Data confidentiality is one of many legal obligations influencing DLT acceptance. The Comprehensive Safeguards Agreement and Additional Protocol, the primary legal agreements underpinning the safeguards system, clearly place an obligation on the IAEA to "take every precaution" [4] to protect the confidentiality of States' safeguards information and maintain a "stringent regime" [7] for safeguards confidentiality. States would need to be reassured that the open nature of DLT did not compromise this fundamental obligation.

There are explicit obligations stated in the Model Subsidiary Arrangement governing safeguards implementation in each State that address the type of information that States must report as well as the expected format, deadlines, and entities responsible for reporting information [9]. As will be discussed later in this chapter, a technology that enables real-time posting of safeguards information raises questions about how States might comply with these obligations and which entities (nuclear operators or State Authorities) would be responsible for posting safeguards-relevant information to the ledger.

Additionally, the IAEA is obligated to perform its safeguards verification activities without placing undue burden on States [4]. While the rapid acceptance of commercial blockchain applications has provided insights about the costs of deployment [10], further research is necessary to determine whether incorporation of DLT into the specialized context of nuclear operations and safeguards verification would pose an undue burden.

Finally, for every technology being considered for safeguards use, the IAEA must work with nuclear operators and State Authorities to evaluate whether the technology can be applied in the State without conflicting with or violating its national laws and regulations. A technology whose functionality depends on wireless communications may not be allowed into certain nuclear facilities whose operating license precludes use of wireless communications.

This strict set of legal requirements presents only one challenge for deploying new technology into the safeguards system. Another set of challenges facing technology acceptance arises due to the complex political environment at the IAEA. The IAEA is a large and dynamic international organization that, as of April 2021, consists of 173 Member States that function by consensus. While its work is largely technical—consisting of monitoring, inspection, and information analysis—the ramifications of any negative finding are highly political. Furthermore, the IAEA is charged with verifying the compliance of the very Member States that oversee it and is staffed with people from across the globe. This type of environment breeds potential political challenges that are often entangled with concerns associated with trust and transparency.

Despite the political tensions inherent in the organization, and because of them, the IAEA's two policy-making bodies, the General Conference and the Board of Governors, ensure the organization acts with the advice and consent of its Member States.

While the Board of Governors consists of representatives of States "most advanced in the technology of atomic energy including the production of source materials," General Conference membership consists of representatives of all Member States [11]. Recognizing their authority and power in the political decision-making process, when considering new safeguards approaches and tools, Member States demand assurance that the new approach or tool will not interfere with the Agency's ability to remain "non-discriminatory," "independent," and "objective" [12–14]. Accordingly, the IAEA dedicates significant attention to the tools and approaches it introduces and uses in the field to ensure its verification activities are aligned with the principles of independence and objectivity [13, 14].

Thus, the political and legal structures argue against replacement of the IAEA as an independent verification body. The IAEA cannot be replaced, nor should it, as it plays a critical role in physically verifying information being reported, either via normal mechanisms or on a distributed ledger. Yet, the first broadly accepted manifestation of DLT, the Bitcoin blockchain, was created to replace the role central authorities such as banks play in managing financial transactions. If the application were to extend to the safeguards context, one might inquire whether DLT would replace the IAEA as the central authority in the system. This tension between DLT's underlying premise and the IAEA's central role in the safeguards system has prompted skepticism within the safeguards community about DLT's role in, and potential value to, safeguards. Furthermore, as an emerging, rapidly evolving technology, DLT's functionality and structure is profoundly confusing and inaccessible to many, further hindering common understanding and appreciation of DLT's potential contributions to safeguards.

Recognizing the structure and evolution of the international safeguards system, the questions that must be addressed before DLT will be accepted by the safeguards community are: (1) Does the legal system allow use of DLT given the requirements for strict confidentiality of data and the central role of the IAEA codified in the safeguards agreements? (2) Does the benefit of utilizing DLT outweigh the costs of implementation? (3) Will Member States accept its deployment? The rest of this chapter will discuss a variety of issues touching on DLT's legal, technical, and political feasibility.

4   Technical Factors Influencing DLT Acceptance

Regarding the first question, we have established in this chapter that the existing legal system presents a rigorous set of parameters for introducing new technologies. Without further exploration and negotiation with States about potential DLT deployment, it remains unclear whether these strict parameters will preclude use of DLT for safeguards. However, there is an opportunity within the legal framework to explore the benefits of new technologies that could improve the effectiveness and efficiency of safeguards verification. A provision within the CSA enables the IAEA to "take full account of technological developments" to improve the efficiency and effectiveness of its activities [4]. As this provision gives the IAEA space within the confines of the legal system to explore potentially beneficial technologies, such exploration must start with an evaluation of the technology's functionality and performance to determine whether States and their operating facilities are likely to accept its use.

Every technology accepted for safeguards use undergoes rigorous testing and evaluation by both the IAEA and Member States' Support Programs, some of which specifically develop and test new equipment and tools for IAEA use. This testing and evaluation process can last many years. For example, the IAEA took approximately five years to develop, test, and deploy two commonly-used surveillance systems, such as the Digital Cherenkov Viewing Device and the Electro-Optical Sealing System. As part of this process:

> the IAEA defines the safeguards needs, coordinates the support programmes, and tests and evaluates the techniques and the resulting equipment developed. All aspects of equipment performance are evaluated, including compliance with specifications, reliability and transportability, and, most importantly, suitability for use by IAEA inspectors in nuclear facilities. The IAEA has an established quality assurance procedure to authorize equipment and software for routine inspection use [15].

Future acceptance of DLT for safeguards use would require a similar evaluation process but may require more extensive consideration since it would not be an incremental improvement like a new seal or verification device. Thus, before making the decision to invest, the IAEA has capitalized on the opportunity to monitor DLT's performance in safeguards and non-safeguards applications through technical meetings involving Member State participation and more intimate discussions with experts in DLT and international safeguards [16–18]. Since any implementation of DLT would likely require investment on the part of Member States it will be necessary to include as many Member States into the discussion as possible. Looking forward, this discussion will likely evolve to focus on questions about the level of acceptance that will be required for successful deployment. For instance, does the use of DLT in safeguards implementation require the participation of all States with safeguards agreements or can it be a subset of all States? Should or can the IAEA impose a specific reporting mechanism on States? As discussed earlier, the answer is likely no, making broad Member State acceptance of DLT acceptance critical.

Thus far, several successful commercial applications of DLT, including, banking, supply chain management, healthcare, real estate, voting, and energy industry, have indicated the technology functions as promised, providing users with greater capabilities in data confidentiality, asset tracking, and auditing [19]. During the last two-to-three years, researchers have begun to develop several prototypes for safeguards use, bolstering the argument that a ledger designed for safeguards purpose also might be technically possible [20, 21]. However, a number of highly visible failures, such as the attack on Coinbase's Ethereum Classic cryptocurrency and the flaw in the smart contract governing the Decentralized Autonomous Organization that enabled the attacker to steal more than USD $60 million in cryptocurrency, have raised questions among skeptical communities of DLT's sustainability as a long-term solution [22].

Despite these failures, the IAEA's increasing challenge of managing, validating, evaluating, and protecting large data streams makes continuing research into information management and data security technologies, including DLT, compelling and necessary. The IAEA was, is, and will continue to be, inundated with data [23, 24]. "Between 2010 and 2017, the amount of nuclear material under IAEA Safeguards increased by over 20%. In 2017, Safeguards staff operated in 182 States, compared with 176 States in 2010, and conducted more than 2000 inspections" [25]. These efforts generate "hundreds of thousands of documents," satellite images, instrument data, and other digitized data, all of which requires careful evaluation and processing in order to draw safeguards conclusions.

From a practical perspective, the IAEA cannot expect to rely solely on humans to perform these tasks while meeting demands for effectiveness and efficiency. The tasks become even more daunting when those same humans are expected to uphold the organization's principles of independence, objectivity, and transparency. For these reasons, the IAEA recognizes the need for advanced computing and analytic techniques to support these analytical efforts and is trying to prepare for the influx of data, as exemplified by its investments in its own information infrastructure [24, 25]. One of the outcomes of these investments is the State Declaration Portal, which is a web-based system that supports secure bi-directional information exchange between States or Regional Authorities and the IAEA. Any future deployment of DLT to support information reporting would need to complement and be integrated into this system [26].

5 Addressing Critical Questions About Deploying DLT for Safeguards

Recognizing the variety of legal, political, and technical factors driving DLT acceptance for safeguards use, and raising questions about its feasibility, researchers in NGOs, academia, and national laboratories have conducted a number of independent, and in some cases, collaborative projects to explore some key questions surrounding DLT deployment [18, 20, 21, 27–32].

Role of the Central Authority

One prominent question involves the role of a distributed ledger to facilitate interactions in a system with a strong central authority. As mentioned earlier in this chapter, public blockchains, such as the Bitcoin blockchain, are potentially contrary to the legal structure of the CSAs in place with NNWSs. The Bitcoin blockchain was designed for peer-to-peer systems that do not need or desire a centralized authority to manage transactions among them. As the central authority managing and verifying safeguards information, the IAEA cannot, and should not, be replaced. However, there are different types of ledgers, namely permissioned ledgers, that could be used appropriately to address aspects of safeguards verification activities involving peer-to-peer interactions. For example, as demonstrated by the Pacific Northwest National Laboratory (PNNL) in 2019, DLT could be used to facilitate certain aspects of the transit matching process, reducing the number of records that would need to be manually matched by the IAEA and improving the general quality of declarations provided to the IAEA [21, 33]. Transit matching is the process for relating or "matching" reports of domestic and international shipments and receipts of nuclear material between facilities within and between countries.

As discussed in the 2017, 2018, and 2019 PNNL reports, and further explored by Sandia National Laboratories, DLT could be used to document international transfers of UF6 cylinders between material balance areas in States while the IAEA verifies the inventory change [21, 28, 30]. A distributed ledger deployed in this way, "could improve the timeliness of detection of diversion of nuclear material through real-time match attempts of all transactions posted to the ledger…inform inspection activities…and increase confidence in IAEA safeguards conclusion" that transferred material was not diverted [21]. The report emphasized that the first two outcomes are supported by other existing computer programs as well as distributed ledgers, but the third outcome pertaining to confidence in safeguards conclusion is "enabled only by the immutability and cryptographic surety that the blockchain provides" [21]. As the transit matching use case demonstrates, it is possible to identify safeguards use cases where the benefits of DLT can be derived without undermining the important function of the IAEA.

The Need v. Benefit of Deploying DLT for Safeguards

Another prominent question under consideration is whether DLT solves a specific verification challenge or adds value in other ways. While imperfect, the international safeguards system functions. The IAEA is able to provide credible assurances that States are honoring their legal obligations using its instruments and verification procedures [34]. Based on research to date, DLT does not solve specific safeguards challenges as much as it adds an overall improvement in the level of security, efficiency, transparency, and trust. Due to the IAEA's budget constraints, there is always an interest in improving the efficiency and effectiveness of safeguards verification activities as well as the timeliness of detection of diverted material or undeclared activities. However, the absence of a clear verification challenge that the technology would resolve raises questions as to whether the costs of exploring, developing, and deploying a complex technology such as DLT for safeguards outweigh the benefits [27].

Impact on Fundamental Safeguards Obligations

A third prominent question focuses on the extent to which fundamental safeguards responsibilities may change as a result of deploying DLT for safeguards purposes. Specifically, the use of computer algorithms and consensus protocols to validate transactions that are posted to the ledger could disrupt the way safeguards information is transmitted and verified today. For example, in States with safeguards agreements in force, nuclear facilities provide safeguards-relevant information to the state authority, which transmits the information to the IAEA via secure email or by hand delivery. This information is provided in standard nuclear material accounting reporting forms in accordance with strict deadlines. The conditions and requirements governing the submission of these reports are clearly established in the State's CSA and corresponding agreements the State negotiates with the IAEA, such as the Subsidiary Arrangement and facility attachments [9]. If DLT were to be deployed to support nuclear material accounting, many of the requirements pertaining to reporting transmission and deadlines might become moot. For example, transactions would be posted on the ledger, potentially precluding the need to submit an official report to the IAEA, as States are currently required to do at regular intervals [4].

This conflict between DLT deployment and State obligations raises an important issue that impact safeguards inspections. Under the current legal framework, without official nuclear material inventory reports to verify, there is no basis for inspection. Additional study is necessary to fully evaluate the political and legal implications of using a cryptographically secure distributed ledger for reporting safeguards information.

6 Evaluating the Value of DLT Deployment for Safeguards: A Summary of Research to Date

With these questions providing context for discussion, research conducted to date has focused on identifying and evaluating potential use cases for deploying DLT without replacing the IAEA or undermining its core verification functions. Early conceptual studies identified transit matching, UF6 cylinder tracking, and nuclear material accounting as promising areas for future examination [18, 20, 21, 27–32]. In addition there has been some work in addressing the possible use of DLT in tracking transfers pursuant to Nuclear Cooperation Agreements [18]. As part of these projects, researchers identified several benefits in using the technology for international safeguards purposes.

The relative transparency of information on a shared distributed ledger is one of the more controversial aspects of DLT as it raises questions around the type of information States can or should share and with whom. Safeguards agreements specify the information the IAEA requires from States to draw safeguards conclusions, and there are few incentives to providing more than what is required to remain compliant with the safeguards agreement. Moreover, States are naturally highly concerned about sharing sensitive nuclear information with anyone other than the IAEA, for both national security and commercial reasons, and expect the IAEA to fulfill its obligation to protect sensitive safeguards information. However, sharing selected information about safeguards transactions, such as the date of the transaction or the countries involved, might help States demonstrate compliance with their safeguards agreements without revealing sensitive information about the nuclear material itself and without adding undue burden to safeguards operations. The fact that ledgers can be designed to share information with stakeholders beyond the IAEA while protecting sensitive information through use of user permissions, encryption, and cryptography creates the potential for monitoring movements of nuclear material in new ways, similar to the use of 'mailbox' declarations for bulk processing facilities but across facilities, potentially increasing confidence in the IAEA's ability to provide assurance that the material remains dedicated to peaceful use.

Another benefit of DLT deployment for safeguards use is that the IAEA might be able to achieve near real-time detection of errors in declarations. The combination of transparency, cryptography and immutability is what makes DLT a unique technology for mitigating distrust while increasing inspector efficiency and effectiveness. While the technology precludes users from manipulating or editing information about past transactions, it might also save inspector time and resources if computer programs running on the ledger could enable automated error detection. It is important to clarify that while many existing computer programs can automate the detection of anomalies, DLT's unique capability comes from combining such automation with the consensus protocols and cryptographic hash functions found only in distributed systems that strengthen the security of the data being posted to the ledger. These are capabilities that existing databases and software programs cannot offer. Integrated in these capabilities is a third benefit of deployment, namely that States and the IAEA might see improvements in data security due to the resilience inherent in a distributed system.

Based on the findings from the various projects emerging from the NGO, academic, and federal communities, several organizations began development of ledger prototypes to establish user requirements and test assumptions within the context of specific use cases. One prototype was the ledger designed by PNNL to explore potential application of DLT in transit matching processes [21].

A second prototype, SLAFKA, and its predecessor, SLUMBAT, were developed by Dr. Edward Obbard, Guntur Dharma Putra and Edward Yu at the University of New South Wales [20]. SLUMBAT was the first blockchain-based demo for nuclear material accounting, demonstrating how the simplest and most direct implementation of an assumed DLT solution for nuclear material accounting would operate. In collaboration with the Henry L. Stimson Center and the Finnish Radiation and Nuclear Safety Authority (STUK) in 2020, Obbard and his team refined and expanded the tool into SLAFKA, the world's first DLT prototype developed for a national nuclear regulator. SLAFKA illustrates how a permissioned blockchain handles safeguards reporting in line with confidentiality of nuclear accounting information in a secure and new way to communicate safeguards data. The prototype is based on Finland's system of accounting and control which uses a centrally stored database called SAFKA. The "SLAFKA" name therefore stands for a "shared ledger SAFKA" [20]. Obbard and his team provide a comparison of the two prototypes in the next chapter.

Lawrence Livermore National Laboratory (LLNL) developed a prototype that explored application of DLT to monitor UF6 cylinders. This researched explored whether DLT might, "provide a digital platform that allows the IAEA and the nuclear industry to improve monitoring the UF6 supply chain, ensure that sensitive material arrives at the final destination through end-user verification, and mitigate pressing proliferation risks by meeting safeguards and export control challenges" [29]. Sandia National Laboratories has also conducted extensive research into different DLT applications, including deployment of DLT for UF6 cylinder tracking in Ethereum, use of DLT for anomaly detection and surety for safeguards data, and deployment DLT as part of an Internet of Things solutions to improve data analytics for safeguards [30–32].

Aside from these prototypes, other use cases involving digital safeguards transactions were examined and ultimately dismissed by PNNL during its early conceptual work [28]. These use cases included the one-way provision of safeguards information, governance processes associated with the noncompliance investigations, and the transmission of data from unattended monitoring and state of health instruments. These use cases were deemed unsuitable for distributed ledgers because they lacked peer-to-peer interactions, thus negating the value of distributed networks, or they lacked sufficient digital data that could be posted on a ledger.

In parallel with prototype development, researchers at the Stimson Center, the Stanley Center for Peace and Security (formerly the Stanley Foundation), and PNNL also turned their attention to the issue of Member State acceptance. During a workshop conducted in Vienna, Austria in the summer of 2019, representatives from state authorities, nuclear operators, the IAEA, the nuclear industry, and blockchain developers gathered to explore a variety of deployment challenges.

During the two-day meeting, participants learned about DLT's evolution and functionality and explored the legal and policy challenges and opportunities for deploying DLT for safeguards use. As documented in the report from that workshop, participants recognized a number of challenges facing DLT acceptance within the safeguards community [27]. For example, there are varying degrees of knowledge, understanding, and access to advanced computing tools among Member States, making broad use of DLT challenging. Participants also discussed Member State concerns about data protection and security, which have led to the establishment of national laws prohibiting electronic transmission of safeguards information. Participants recognized that because many States deliver their safeguards reports in hardcopy, on CDs, or USBs, they would be unlikely to use DLT for safeguards purpose, regardless of IAEA interest in the technology. Participants also discussed the legal framework that governs any future DLT deployment. They concluded that any ledger used for safeguards purposes will need to be integrated into a well-established technical infrastructure.

On a positive note, workshop participants also recognized several opportunities that could support DLT deployment for safeguards use. First, the potential for DLT acceptance improves once Member States are educated about how the technology works. This finding became evident after participants were surveyed before and after the workshop. Survey findings showed a distinct shift in perspective about DLT once participants learned how the technology works. With greater understanding about DLT's functionality, participants also recognized that DLT offers something above and beyond existing information management systems at the IAEA, namely interoperability among systems and frontloading inspection efforts, without replacing the important regulatory function of performing physical verification of nuclear inventories. From a political perspective, participants noted that DLT platforms would not change what safeguards information is reported or undermine the extent to which it is protected from manipulation or theft, two of the most politically charged issues for the international safeguards community.

7 Summary

Research into DLT's use for safeguards continues as States grapple with questions about deployment costs, political acceptability, and system integration. Its ultimate success will depend on leaders in the community who are willing to take the first step in developing and demonstrating how the technology can be used to benefit the IAEA, State regulatory authorities, and nuclear operators. These pioneers will help inform future research and define user requirements, making broader access to the technology more likely in the future.

References

1. Krikorian S (2020) Preliminary nuclear power facts and figures for 2019. In: The international atomic energy agency department of nuclear energy. https://www.iaea.org/newscenter/news/preliminary-nuclear-power-facts-and-figures-for-2019. Accessed 29 Mar 2020
2. International Atomic Energy Agency (2021) More on safeguards agreements. https://www.iaea.org/topics/safeguards-legal-framework/more-on-safeguards-agreements. Accessed 29 Mar 2021
3. Treaty on the Non-Proliferation of Nuclear Weapons (1968) Full text. https://www.un.org/disarmament/wmd/nuclear/npt/text/. Accessed 29 Mar 2020
4. International Atomic Energy Agency (1972) The structure and content of agreements between the agency and states required in connection with the treaty on the non-proliferation of nuclear weapons. INFCIRC/153. Para 6. https://www.iaea.org/sites/default/files/publications/documents/infcircs/1972/infcirc153.pdf. Accessed 2 April 2020
5. International Atomic Energy Agency (2016) IAEA safeguards: delivering effective nuclear verification for world peace. https://www.iaea.org/sites/default/files/16/08/iaea_safeguards_introductory_leaflet.pdf. Accessed 2 Apr 2020
6. International Atomic Energy Agency (2015) IAEA safeguards: serving nuclear non-proliferation. https://www.iaea.org/sites/default/files/safeguards_web_june_2015_1.pdf. Accessed 5 Apr 2020
7. International Atomic Energy Agency (1997) Model protocol additional to the agreements between states and the International Atomic Energy Agency for the application of safeguards. INFCIRC/540. https://www.iaea.org/sites/default/files/infcirc540.pdf. Accessed 5 Apr 2020
8. International Atomic Energy Agency (2012) Review of management and administration in the International Atomic Energy Agency. JIU/REP/2012/13/Rev.1. https://www.unjiu.org/sites/www.unjiu.org/files/jiu_document_files/products/en/reports-notes/JIU%20Products/JIU_REP_2012_13_Rev.1.pdf. Accessed 2 Apr 2020
9. International Atomic Energy Agency (2017) Subsidiary arrangement to the agreement between the government of _____ and the international atomic energy agency for the application of

safeguards in connection with the treaty on the nonproliferation of nuclear weapons. 1974-03-12. https://www.iaea.org/sites/default/files/sg-fm-1170-subsidiary-arrangement-code-1-9.pdf. Accessed 26 Apr 2020.

10. Takyar A (2020) How to determine the cost of blockchain implementation. LeewayHertz. https://www.leewayhertz.com/cost-of-blockchain-implementation/. Accessed 15 Jul 2020
11. International Atomic Energy Agency (1957) Statute of the IAEA. https://www.iaea.org/about/statute#a1-6. Accessed 12 July 2020
12. Häckel E (2020) Verification: the politics of the unpolitical. In: Niemeyer I, Dreicer M, Stein G (eds) Nuclear non-proliferation and arms control verification. Springer, Cham
13. International Atomic Energy Agency (2013) The conceptualization and development of safeguards implementation at the state level. GOV/2013/38. https://armscontrollaw.files.wordpress.com/2012/06/state-level-safeguards-concept-report-august-2013.pdf. Accessed 29 Mar 2020
14. International Atomic Energy Agency (2014) Fact sheet #3: information relevant to the IAEA General Conference. Topic: safeguards resolution. http://www.nonproliferation.org/wp-content/uploads/2014/09/2014_IAEA_GC_QA_Safeguards.pdf. Accessed 29 Mar 2020
15. International Atomic Energy Agency (2011) Safeguards techniques and equipment: 2011 Edition. international nuclear verification Series No. 1 (Rev.2). pp 2–3. https://www-pub.iaea.org/MTCD/Publications/PDF/nvs1_web.pdf. Accessed 2 April 2020
16. International Atomic Energy Agency (2017) Emerging technologies workshop: trends and implications for safeguards. https://www.iaea.org/sites/default/files/18/09/emerging-technologies-130217.pdf. Accessed 10 Apr 2020
17. Mutluer A (2020) Experts gather in Vienna to discuss the impact of emerging technologies on nuclear verification. https://www.iaea.org/newscenter/news/experts-gather-in-vienna-to-discuss-the-impact-of-emerging-technologies-on-nuclear-verification. Accessed 16 Apr 2020
18. Stimson Center Salons conducted between 2018 and 2020
19. Business Insider (2020) The growing list of applications and use cases of blockchain technology in business and life. Business Insider Intelligence. https://www.businessinsider.com/blockchain-technology-applications-use-cases. Accessed 2 Apr 2020
20. Obbard EG, Le L, Yu E (2018) Evaluation of a blockchain based nuclear materials accounting platform in Australia. In: Paper presented at the IAEA symposium on international safeguards: building future safeguards capabilities, Vienna, Austria, 5–8 Nov 2018
21. Frazar SL et al (2019) Transit matching blockchain prototype. PNNL-29527. Pacific Northwest National Laboratory, Richland
22. Orcutt M (2019). Once hailed as unhackable, blockchains are now getting hacked. MIT Technol Rev. https://www.technologyreview.com/s/612974/once-hailed-as-unhackable-blockchains-are-now-getting-hacked/ Accessed 5 Apr 2020
23. Ferguson M and Norman C (2018). All-source information acquisition and analysis in the IAEA Department of Safeguards. In: Paper presented at the IAEA symposium on international safeguards: building future safeguards capabilities, Vienna, Austria, 5–8 Nov 2018. https://www.osti.gov/etdeweb/servlets/purl/21490222. Accessed 10 Apr 2020
24. International Atomic Energy Agency (2017) MOSAIC: the modernization of safeguards information technology. https://www.iaea.org/sites/default/files/17/01/mosaic.pdf. Accessed 10 Apr 2020
25. International Atomic Energy Agency (2018). IAEA completes 3-year project to modernize safeguards IT system. https://www.iaea.org/newscenter/pressreleases/iaea-completes-3-year-project-to-modernize-safeguards-it-system. Accessed 10 Apr 2020
26. International Atomic Energy Agency (2021) State declaration portal. https://www.iaea.org/resources/databases/state-declarations-portal. Accessed 7 May 2021
27. Frazar SL et al (2019) Evaluating blockchain for safeguards: report on workshop findings. Pacific Northwest National Laboratory, Richland, WA. https://www.stimson.org/2020/evaluating-member-state-acceptance-of-blockchain-for-nuclear-safeguards/. Accessed 17 Apr 2020
28. Frazar SL et al (2017) Exploratory study on potential safeguards applications for shared ledger technology. PNNL-26229. Pacific Northwest National Laboratory, Richland, WA

29. Gasser P (2019) A Distributed Ledger Technology (DLT) approach to monitoring UF6 cylinders: lessons learned from tradelens. LLNL-CONF-777061. https://www.osti.gov/servlets/purl/1543077. Accessed 26 Apr 2020
30. Pattengale N, Farley D (2019) Prototype distributed tedger Technology of UF6 cylinder tracking in Ethereum. unpublished, Sandia National Laboratories
31. Peter-Stein N et al (2020) Development of novel approaches to anomaly detection and surety for safeguards data—year one results, SAND2020–5665C, Sandia National Laboratories
32. Farley, D et al (2018) Industrial internet-of-things & data analytics for nuclear power & safeguards" SAND2018–12807, Sandia National Laboratories
33. Frazar SL et al (2018) Evaluating safeguards use cases for blockchain applications. PNNL-28050. Pacific Northwest National Laboratory, Richland, WA
34. International Atomic Energy Agency. Safeguards Implementation Reports. Available at: iaea.org/publications/reports. Accessed 9 September 2021.

Blockchain Tools for Nuclear Safeguards

Edward Obbard, Edward Yu, and Guntur Dharma Putra

SLUMBAT and SLAFKA are a minimal demonstration and a prototype blockchain solution for nuclear material accounting. This chapter explains how these two demonstrations of DLT for nuclear safeguards met the requirements for the recording, reporting, and access control of information for nuclear material in two different States. The researchers' reflections on developing and demonstrating these solutions are presented, followed by a discussion of what should be addressed for future iterations.

1 Background—from NUMBAT to SLUMBAT to SLAFKA

The amount of nuclear material accounting-related information being managed, processed, analyzed, and stored by the International Atomic Energy Agency (IAEA) has increased dramatically since its establishment in the 1950s. As a result, the IAEA continues to seek new technologies that can help improve the efficiency and effectiveness of its information analysis and management systems. Its investment in the MOSAIC project between 2015 and 2018 is a prominent example of the IAEA's efforts to improve its own information infrastructure in this regard [1]. Member States are also playing a key role in the development and testing of new technologies that

E. Obbard (✉) · E. Yu
School of Mechanical and Manufacturing Engineering, University of New South Wales, Kensington, Australia
e-mail: e.obbard@unsw.edu.au

G. D. Putra
School of Computer Science and Engineering, University of New South Wales, Kensington, Australia

© Springer Nature Switzerland AG 2021   37
C. Vestergaard (ed.), *Blockchain for International Security*,
Advanced Sciences and Technologies for Security Applications,
https://doi.org/10.1007/978-3-030-86240-4_4

can improve the efficiency and effectiveness of nuclear material information management. This chapter discusses and compares two such technologies, SLUMBAT and SLAFKA, that were developed by researchers at the University of New South Wales (UNSW) in Australia.

SLUMBAT and SLAFKA are two separate but related systems that demonstrated how distributed ledger technology (DLT) can be used for collecting, storing, and reporting nuclear material accounting data to the IAEA. SLUMBAT is a demonstration based on the functionality of Australia's Nuclear Material Balances and Tracking (NUMBAT) tool. SLAFKA was developed leveraging lessons learned from the SLUMBAT design and development process and, from the regulator's user perspective, provides the Finnish national regulator with at least the functionality of their existing nuclear material accounting database.

NUMBAT was developed by the Australian Safeguards and Non-Proliferation Office (ASNO) to serve as a digital web-based nuclear material accounting and reporting system [2]. NUMBAT eliminated transcription errors in reporting through use of dropdown menu choices and saved time by allowing permit holders to record material inventory and inventory changes through an online portal. The information uploaded into NUMBAT is formatted for upload to the IAEA State Declaration Portal, which was one new outcome of the MOSAIC project.

In 2018, UNSW researchers initiated a project in collaboration with ASNO to test how a tool based on DLT would compare to another digital but centralized national safeguards information management system [3]. Ultimately, the Shared Ledger version of NUMBAT or 'SLUMBAT' became one of the earliest practical examples of how DLT might be used for nuclear material accounting purposes [4].

In 2019, Finland's Radiation and Nuclear Safety Authority (STUK), the Stimson Center, a non-governmental organization in Washington, D.C., and UNSW collaborated on an effort to adapt SLUMBAT into an application for Finland's safeguards program [5]. The name 'SLAFKA' references STUK's existing nuclear material accounting database, SAFKA, and represents another prominent and early example of how DLT might be deployed for safeguards use.

This chapter describes and compares SLUMBAT and SLAFKA 's development process and design requirements and discusses their impact in terms of nuclear safeguards. The chapter examines the crucial functions for the implementation of nuclear material accounting tools, which are how to organize records and reports of nuclear material information, confidentiality, and data permissions. SLUMBAT and SLAFKA's deployment illustrate how these functions have been achieved. The chapter ends with some consideration of potential next steps in the research.

2   SLUMBAT—Initial Development

One of the biggest drivers behind SLUMBAT's development was the need to reduce the likelihood that a State might falsify records to divert nuclear material to a clandestine nuclear program. Falsification of records appears in roughly half of diversion scenarios examined [6]. The underlying premise behind SLUMBAT's development was that a DLT-enabled platform would provide an immutable ledger of nuclear material accounting information among permit holders, the State Authority, and the IAEA, which would make the falsification of electronic records in a diversion attempt significantly more difficult.

Specifically, SLUMBAT was designed on the principle that every physical movement, transformation, or modification relating to physical batches of nuclear material should be accompanied by a representative blockchain transaction on the digital asset. The assumption is that once such information is captured, then it cannot be lost on the append-only ledger. A participant can extract data from the shared ledger at any time to compile the required reports, the content of which will be based on their access privileges.

SLUMBAT was built using the Kubernetes API [7] in Hyperledger Composer Playground, an application development framework on top of the Hyperledger Fabric suite that assists the development of Hyperledger Fabric applications. Hyperledger Fabric is a private, permissioned blockchain framework developed by an IBM-led consortium under the auspices of the Linux Foundation's Hyperledger project. Hyperledger Fabric was chosen because its permissioned architecture provides the required ability to define permissions for different users to see and edit only subsets of information stored on a shared ledger.

SLUMBAT development followed Agile conventions, in particular the writing of user stories as a first step in creating a new piece of software [8]. A user story creates a contextual association between a stakeholder, a requirement, and a benefit of the product. It represents the smallest unit of work and end requirement from a user perspective. SLUMBAT user stories included reporting nuclear material inventories, domestic shipments of nuclear material between facilities via an intermediary transport provider, and making corrections to errors in the reported inventories. An example of a SLUMBAT user story, which relates to a license holder controlling accounting area 'KMP_A' is,

'As owner of KMP_A, I want to report that I received a batch of nuclear materials, so that my State safeguards regulator is aware of this.'

Each user story translates to one or more implicit software requirements for the demo. Specifically, this first user story implies that the user is associated with a specific accounting area, over which they exercise a degree of authority; they will need to initiate a blockchain transaction on receipt of nuclear material into their accounting area, and this new information will be visible to their State regulator. One user story for the State safeguards regulator is,

'As the State safeguards regulator, I want to identify if there were any shipper-receiver differences, so I can investigate them further.'

The second user story implies the State regulator has a historical, global view of transactions among their licensees, which it consults to identify changes in inventory for further investigation. A user story written from the point of view of the IAEA, relating to the safeguards definition of a nuclear material accounting area, the Material Balance Area (MBA), is,

'As the IAEA, I want to identify any modifications in the amount of material held in MBAs, so that I am assured that State safeguards regulator(s) can't reverse transactions to hide attempted diversion when I hold an inspection.'

The third user story escalates this superuser type of oversight to an international level, implying the IAEA occupies a third layer in the user hierarchy above the national regulators; it also sets a requirement that all users in the system are bound by an append-only data storage system such that transactions cannot be undone by the participants.

SLUMBAT scope was initially limited to transfer of nuclear material between permit holders in a single country. The resulting software was demonstrated across two sessions, by a total of four local professionals in nuclear safeguards in either a license holder or regulator capacity [3]. Participants in the sessions were assigned roles, either as a regulator, or as one of two license-holders. Phenomenological evaluation was performed by interviewing participants on their experiences during and after the demonstration. The evaluation identified several features that would be worth adding in future versions of the tool: the ability to capture rebatching at nuclear facilities, sender-receiver transactions, flagging of anomalies, and querying and report generation.

Querying and report generation were later implemented in SLAFKA, while rebatching along with sender-receiver transactions and the addition of a second State regulator to represent international transactions, was pursued along with a second SLUMBAT demo, described below.

2.1   SLUMBAT 2.0—Transit Matching Demonstration

Invitees at an international workshop, drawn from the IAEA and the safeguards community in Member States, including State authorities, national missions, blockchain companies, research institutions, and international organizations took part in a demo of SLUMBAT 2.0 [9]. This demonstration involved the roles of an enrichment plant in Country B (ENR-B), a transporter in County B (TR-B), the state regulatory authority of Country A (SRA-A), and a fuel fabrication plant in Country A (FFP-A). Figure 1 shows a schematic of these participants.

Rebatching is the re-naming of a batch of nuclear material, including possible redistribution of the contents of batches to match processing requirements in a nuclear facility [10]. Execution of the following steps in a nuclear material supply chain demonstrated how a DLT nuclear material accounting system could track inventory changes during a receipt of nuclear material and a rebatching operation:

1.   ENR-B consigns two batches of nuclear materials to FFP-A via TR-B.
2.   SRA-A observes that nuclear material is destined for holder FFP-A.

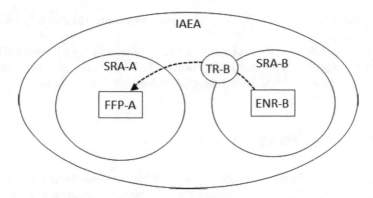

Fig. 1 The participants in a SLUMBAT 2.0 demonstration

3. FFP-A observes that nuclear material is destined to itself.
4. TR-B hands over the batches to FFP-A so that it can take possession.
5. FFP-A takes possession of batches, so that regulator SRA-A and the IAEA can see this change.
6. FFP-A combines the batches and modifies their descriptions, with consistent enrichment and mass attributes.
7. SRA-A sees that rebatching had taken place, allowing it to verify this against inspection results; SRA-A also knows that the inventory change is visible to the IAEA, allowing SRA-A to fulfill its reporting obligations.

A batch of nuclear material in SLUMBAT is a non-fungible, enduring asset with a unique identity, registered on the shared ledger. Metadata associated with the batch provides the information that would need to be reported, were it to constitute a permit holder's nuclear material inventory—this includes element type, element, weight, location, and other descriptors (described further in Sect. 4). To transfer batch ownership during shipment and receipt of nuclear material, in a way that restricts edit permissions during transit, batches in SLUMBAT 2.0 included metadata fields to specify both a current owner and a destined owner, and a field called 'Handed Off' which could be set True/False.

For step (1), above, to consign nuclear material, ENR-B can modify its own batch, updating current owner to TR-B and destined owner to FFP-A. According to rules implemented in SLUMBAT, this batch then becomes visible to SRA-A and FFP-A because the destined owner matches their jurisdiction and name, respectively. The transaction used by the transporter at (4) to hand-off the batch to FFP-A causes the Handed Off attribute to be set True. FFP-A can then execute a Receipt Domestic transaction on the batch, updating current owner to its own name, being the organization already named in the destined owner field.

Crucially, the transporter's role precludes it from all other transactions, and the recipient FFP-A must execute the receipt-domestic transaction to take position of the batch, before they can make any other changes. Having taken ownership (5), FFP-A is immediately recorded as the new owner, and this is visible to SRA-A, because of their jurisdiction over FFP-A. Any subsequent rebatching (6) can only take place after this transfer.

Because each distinct step is clearly enforced, and can only be executed by the batch owner, regulatory agencies can consult (7) the enduring record of how the content and naming of batches was changed, in a step-by-step fashion.

2.2   SLUMBAT Outcomes

SLUMBAT showed how a DLT solution could deliver the fundamental functionality and nuclear material accounting transactions for nuclear safeguards. From a user perspective, SLUMBAT seemed to be practical and suggested real benefits in transit-matching and diversion detection, which went beyond the benefits of moving from a paper or email-based system to an electronic reporting portal as experienced during NUMBAT's deployment.

The SLUMBAT transit matching demonstration showed how DLT could mitigate an existing challenge to nuclear material accounting that occurs when a license holder simultaneously logs receipt of a consignment and re-batches it to new containers, in the same reporting period. Combining transactions together creates additional work for the State regulator and for the IAEA in correctly matching the consignments because the material reported as received can be different to the report of the shipment from the consignor. Though originally conceived as potential mitigation to a diversion scenario that involves falsification, demonstrating this operational advantage of a DLT system advanced the discussion of DLT in nuclear safeguards to place more focus on potential benefits, rather than 'fixing' shortcomings of current reporting systems, which are already considered by most key stakeholders to be fit for purpose [9].

Finally, the SLUMBAT development process created a conceptual framework for translating international regulatory structures used for nuclear safeguards to the practical considerations for a DLT software implementation [4]. This successful experience validated the delineation of jurisdictions and roles of participants in a safeguards ecosystem into a permissioning table, which was used to set up the access controls, and the fundamentally batch-centric structure of the reporting system. These features—recording and reporting of information and confidentiality and permission—were addressed during the design and development of the SLAFKA demo and are further described in the following section.

3 SLAFKA

The objective of the SLAFKA project was to build a DLT-based nuclear materials accounting prototype, modelled on the user requirements of STUK; their stakeholders; the regional safeguards inspectorate, the European Atomic Energy Community (Euratom), and the IAEA. An important aspect of the prototype was to provide a tool for the familiarization and education of users on the characteristics of a possible DLT solution in the unique context of their work—an objective which in part derived from key findings of the workshop where SLUMBAT 2.0 was demonstrated [9].

Like SLUMBAT, SLAFKA was built in Hyperledger Fabric, which offers features that are attractive to the nuclear safeguards use case to preserve the confidentiality of blockchain data and restrict user permissions over reading and writing data [11]. In addition, Hyperledger Fabric allows flexible customizations that would help to achieve design goals in SLAFKA. For example, SLAFKA demands a stringent rule of membership, which dictates that all participants must be known in advance—a requirement that cannot be achieved by any public blockchain. Below, the salient features of Hyperledger Fabric, chaincode, channels, endorsement policies, peer nodes, and endorsement policies, are briefly described.

Chaincodes are computer programs written to define the logic behind every operation in Hyperledger Fabric. To verify the validity of chaincode operations, each chaincode execution is validated by peers in the network.

Channels are virtual blockchain networks sitting on top of an actual blockchain network. Channels allow a subgroup of a blockchain network's participants who are executing transactions in common to process these transactions without depending on entities outside the group. This feature can be used to create a separate ledger accessible only to those belonging to the subgroup.

Endorsement policies allow a proposed transaction in Hyperledger Fabric to be endorsed by a specified number of predetermined peer nodes, which in turn helps to preserve the privacy of transactions, as the transactions will only be broadcast to authorized participants.

Peer nodes are computer nodes that host copies of the nuclear material data in a shared immutable database (the blockchain ledger). Peer nodes also store and execute chaincode.

The *Ordering service* organizes each endorsed transaction on a time basis and issues the instruction to peer nodes to store them as an immutable record in the ledger.

In SLAFKA, the fundamental element of the network is a peer node run by a participant. To make SLAFKA operational, a channel is created in the network between all SLAFKA participants for communication purposes, which each peer node can join.

Rules regulating how proposed transactions must be verified and endorsed are defined in the endorsement policy. SLAFKA's endorsement policy states that a transaction proposed by a nuclear operator undergoes verification by at least one regulator's peer node to avoid false or erroneous change made by the operator. Verification involves checking the requested transaction for consistency against the current state of the ledger and checking the signature of the operator peer node requesting the transaction to confirm their identity. To execute a verified transaction, the nuclear regulator node runs the ordering service.

To enable convenient interaction between users and the DLT system, and to provide graphical representation of the structure and procedures for SLAFKA transactions, an additional web-based application was created. The web-based application is administered by the national nuclear regulator as a trusted intermediary, by running a separate web-server instance connected to the DLT system, through which a user may send requests for queries and transactions to SLAFKA. The web-based application provides a graphical user interface (GUI), shown in Fig. 2, which is displayed to individual users via their web browser. SLAFKA participants can invoke SLAFKA transactions via the SLAFKA GUI on any web browser after authenticating themselves. As such, the interactions mostly involve visual interaction, without the need of manually typing SLAFKA commands.

Operators who may not be familiar with different types of information technology can use SLAFKA by inputting changes in their nuclear material inventories into the web interface, as is normally done in their day-to-day settings. As a means of authentication, individual users provide preapproved login credentials, such as username and password, when they open the web-application for the first time. Appropriate credentials identify the user and whether they belong to certain nuclear operators or regulators.

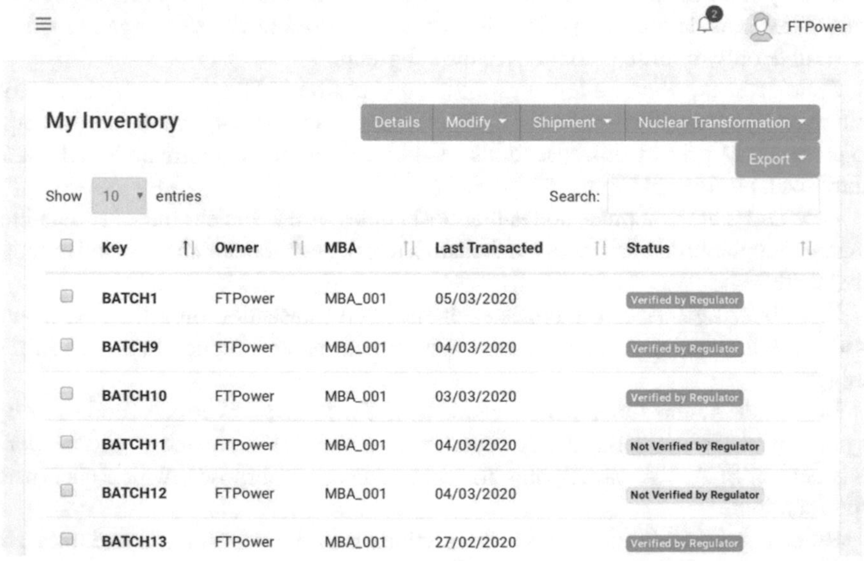

Fig. 2 View of the SLAFKA GUI from a nuclear operator called FTPower

SLAFKA performed functions that were not in scope for SLUMBAT and advanced the demonstration of DLT for nuclear material accounting in three respects:

SLAFKA was developed for a specific end-user organization, in a country which uses nuclear energy and soon will use deep geological disposal. Possible disruption to existing practices caused by the introduction of a DLT system was softened by producing a solution that prioritized compliance with existing legislation and ease of use for end-users, many of whom were affiliated with the nuclear regulator.

SLAFKA was built on a commodity blockchain platform with the technical scope of the implementation significantly greater than SLUMBAT, including an intuitive web-based GUI and secure cloud deployment with end-to-end encryption.

SLAFKA introduced features previously identified during trials as missing from SLUMBAT, including querying, report generation and verification of batches by the regulator.

4 Recording and Reporting Nuclear Material Accounting Information

A material accounting solution must collect and store the data necessary to generate reports for the IAEA and Euratom. The content of safeguards reporting for Finland is based on Commission Regulation (Euratom) No. 302/2005 [12]. Both Annexes III-V of the Euratom regulations and the IAEA's Model Subsidiary Arrangement Code 10 (Code 10) [13] specify the three types of reports to be made by State regulatory authorities: Inventory Change Reports (ICRs), Physical Inventory Listings (PILs) and Material Balance Reports (MBRs). ICRs report changes in inventory, PILs report the result of physical inventories, and MBRs provide aggregate material balances for each type of material at specified locations [14].

SLUMBAT and SLAFKA manage safeguards data by representing nuclear material in standardized batch units and by allowing attribute modification to each batch. Batches in SLUMBAT and SLAFKA are digital assets which are possessed by holder peers and can be exchanged between them. Batches can be modified but have a unique, lasting identity and are not fungible. An alternative approach has been to make the shipping and receiving records digital assets with nuclear material transactions recorded as data objects of these records [15]. Modifications are made primarily by the nuclear operators, or permit holders, who are transacting the batches, and there is little active role for the regulators in these transactions except for observing and periodically making inspections to provide physical verification and ensure data accuracy. The execution of transactions on nuclear material inventories merges with and replaces the action of submitting reports about the inventory.

Key batch attributes for SLAFKA are listed in Table 1. A batch is not tied permanently to a permit holder, but rather has a current owner, and an inventory location—a Key Measurement Point (KMP) and a Material Balance Area (MBA). The batch contains the fields required by IAEA and Euratom regulations for compiling reports.

SLAFKA has 13 distinct transactions, which are summarized in Table 2. Inventory change transactions alter the state of a batch, including batch creation and batch modification. All the inventory change transactions reset the verified-by-regulator

Table 1 SLAFKA batch attributes

Batch attributes	Description
Batch_ID	A unique numerical identity for each batch, e.g., 'BATCH_001'
MBA, KMP, materialForm, materialContainer, materialState, elementCategory, elementWeight, etc	IAEA reporting and Euratom regulation terms
U235 isotope weight	Isotope weight of U-235
Measurement	Basis on which the quantity of nuclear material reported was established
Verified by regulator	Binary field indicating whether the batch has been inspected and verified by nuclear regulator
Owner	The current owner of the batch
Destined to	Whom a batch is being sent to; blank if batch is not in transit
Comment	Record of dated comments made throughout life of batch
Last transacted	Date of last transaction made on batch

Table 2 Summary of SLAFKA transactions

Type	Category	Transaction
Inventory change	Batch creation	Material production
		Receipt foreign
		Nuclear transformation (loss)
		Nuclear transformation (production)
	Batch ownership modification	Shipment domestic
		Receipt domestic
		Shipment foreign
	General batch modification	Change location
		Change attributes
		Remeasurement
		Rebatching
Non-inventory change	Non-inventory change	Query
		Verify

attribute (row 6, Table 1) to False and update the last-transacted attribute (row 10, Table 1). The possible categories of inventory change transactions include batch creations, modifying ownership, and other modification without modifying ownership. The inventory change transactions can be executed by any holders of nuclear material.

Non-inventory change transactions are for viewing and verifying the state of a user's inventory and do not incur changes in the inventory of a particular user. The SLAFKA query transaction reads the current state of user's inventory and returns a list of batches within the user's access privilege. For regulators, the list of batches also includes the MBA history of the batch and the trail of rebatching comments. In this way the query transaction allows a regulator to establish provenance of batches. Holders are only able to see batch provenance as it relates to their own MBAs. The query transaction is called frequently for operation of the SLAFKA GUI, providing a means to show batches that are visible to a particular user, updating the GUI prior to executing other inventory change transactions.

The verify transaction alters the verified-by-regulator attribute to indicate that the batch has been inspected and verified. All participants can execute query transactions, while only the regulators and super-regulator can execute a verify transaction. In the current version of SLAFKA, there is only one kind of regulator verification. However, the verification process could be extended to show verification by different authorities, with each one having sole permission to set their corresponding verified-by-regulator attribute.

5   Confidentiality and Permissioning

This section describes how the SLUMBAT Framework for access controls and permissioning in a DLT nuclear materials accounting system was first developed, and then applied in SLAFKA.

In its most basic form, DLT implies the sharing of an authoritative ledger between participants. INFCIRC/135 [16] requires the IAEA to "protect commercial and industrial secrets and other confidential information coming to its knowledge," in its implementation of nuclear safeguards. Such conditions mean that locations and movements of nuclear material should only be known to the parties involved and the regulatory authorities. Therefore, for non-fungible assets, it is necessary to define the access permissions for each of these at an individual level. Permissioned blockchains such as Hyperledger Fabric permit different roles for participants.

Developing SLUMBAT required definition of participant access controls at a fine level. The original SLUMBAT access control list was built up from the researchers' knowledge of the salient regulatory relationships, combined with user feedback from the SLUMBAT demos, and by considering in turn the jurisdiction and role of each participant.

Jurisdiction of a SLUMBAT participant relates to which other participants a given peer can observe and interact with. It is the range of oversight the peer has over participants.

Role of a participant describes what batch information about nuclear material inventories it can access or edit on the ledger. And it is defined by the range of transactions available to a participant to carry out on batches or other participants.

In SLUMBAT there were three types of participants: nuclear material holders, representing permit holders who possess nuclear materials, regulators, representing national regulatory agencies, and a single super-regulator, representing the IAEA. All nuclear material accounting information was shared between peers at or very soon after the time it was added to the platform. Reading and writing this data using smart contracts then follows rules set out by the access control list as listed in Table 3.

Participants named in row 1 (columns 1–4) have permissions as stated in the same column over another participant listed in column 5; e.g., 'Holders can READ Regulators'.

The super-regulator, in the fourth column, has far-reaching access to read information, but not to create or to edit batches. All participants can view metadata pertaining

Table 3 Selected entries from the SLUMBAT access control list [4]

Holders	Transport providers	Regulators	Super-regulator	Permission over	
READ	None	READ	READ, CREATE	Regulators	Jurisdiction descriptors
READ	READ	READ, CREATE, UPDATE	None	Holders	
READ	READ	READ, UPDATE	READ, UPDATE	Self	
READ	None	READ	READ	Own transaction history	
None	None	READ	READ	All transaction history	
READ, UPDATE	READ, UPDATE*	N/A	N/A	Own Batches	Role descriptors
READ, UPDATE**	None	N/A	N/A	Destined Batches	
None	None	READ, CREATE, UPDATE[a]	READ	All Batches in jurisdiction	

*SLUMBAT transport providers can only edit one attribute of batches, the handed-off (true/false) attribute, which when True allows the new owner to update batch details. **Only if the batch has been 'handed-off.' [a]End user feedback during SLUMBAT development suggested that the Regulator should retain editing privileges over batches in their jurisdiction—privileges that were later revoked in SLAFKA

Table 4 Participants in SLAFKA and their corresponding type in the SLUMBAT framework

Name	Type	Jurisdiction	Note
FT Power	Holder	National	Commercial nuclear plant operator
PVO	Holder	National	Commercial nuclear plant operator
DGROrg	Holder	National	Organization running a deep geological repository
FINREG	Regulator	National	National regulating authority (STUK)
RegionREG	Regulator	Regional	Regional regulating authority, (Euratom)
WorldREG	Super-regulator	International	International regulator (IAEA)

to themselves (row 4); however, holders and transporters cannot edit their own details, synonymous with the idea that the regulator must license a holder by creating an identity for it in the operational DLT system. A national regulator's jurisdiction implies that it can update and create holders within this (row 3), however the super-regulator cannot create or modify holders in the jurisdiction of a regulator (also row 3).

A SLUMBAT holder can issue transactions on batches if it owns the batch (row 7), or if it is the destined owner of a batch that has been handed over by a transport provider (row 8). Holders cannot access data relating to the batches of other holders (row 9). These rules mediate rebatching and facilitate transit matching (Scct. 2.2).

End-user feedback during SLUMBAT 2.0 development suggested that the regulator should retain update privileges over batches in their jurisdiction (row 9). Note that this does not imply the regulator can circumvent the append-only nature of blockchain records, and any changes made would still be immutable, and auditable. In the original SLUMBAT 1.0 demo, the regulator would use this authority as one way to create new batches inside its jurisdiction, at the same time as authorizing an international import of nuclear material, from outside the system.

Table 4 below presents a summary of participants in SLAFKA. These include three operators, who are FTPower, PVO, and DGROrg. FTPower and PVO represent nuclear power plants and DGROrg represents the Finnish deep geological repository. Both STUK and Euratom oversee Finnish nuclear operators as part of their jurisdiction, and they both have roles in inspecting and verifying Finnish nuclear material. SLAFKA therefore had to provide simultaneous oversight roles to these two regulators. FINREG represents the national regulator, RegionREG the regional authority (Euratom) and WorldREG is the international regulator (the IAEA).

Table 4 also shows how the SLUMBAT Framework could readily be adapted to implementation in SLAFKA. FTPower, PVO, and DGROrg are equivalent to SLUMBAT holders. FINReg and RegionREG are both SLUMBAT regulators and WorldREG is a super-regulator in terms of the SLUMBAT Framework. Table 4 is related to Table 3 via the holder, regulator, super-regulator terminology of the SLUMBAT Framework. Noteworthy, was how the addition of a third regulator did not disrupt the overall framework and was fully compatible with the existing structure; also, how the differing roles of the nuclear operators ranging from deep geological repository to nuclear power plant were readily integrated.

On a technical level, permissioning in SLAFKA was implemented by building access control mechanisms into the chaincode. For example, the chaincode transaction for transferring ownership of a batch checks whether the user proposing it is in a list of approved holder nodes and has permission to transact that batch. SLAFKA also checks whether the node calling the transaction matches that of the owner of the asset. Equally, a node seeking to read information about a particular batch would execute a query transaction for reading batch attributes—and the chaincode for the Query transaction will only execute if the peer node proposing the transaction meets conditions specified in the chaincode, i.e., being a holder and being an owner of the batch.

The special role of the regulator in SLUMBAT in authorizing batch creation was removed in SLAFKA, and the holders have sole ability to create batches, with the regulators as observers and verifiers of transactions. Therefore, the DLT data ecosystem mirrors reality where the regulators and the super-regulators have diminished access privileges, and arguably limited role, compared to the holders, who can edit any attributes of their own batches. However, regulators in SLAFKA retain far greater privileges than holders concerning visibility over batches, reflecting their wider jurisdiction. Regulators in SLAFKA can see details of any batch within their jurisdiction, compared to the narrow visibility possessed by holders, which is limited to batches either currently owned by or consigned to the holder.

As regulators, SLAFKA's RegionREG and FINREG have permission to query and show provenance of all batches in their jurisdiction. They also have the special regulatory role of being able to verify batches through a physical inspection, which the holders do not have. The ability of batch verification ensures that the data stored on the ledger is accurate, in the same way that safeguards inspections verify the content of reporting to IAEA at present. Hence, inaccurate batch data would remain in an 'unverified' status following a physical inventory verification, thereby flagging the relevant data for correction and possible further measures.

Jurisdiction can be detailed in its implementation, such that a super-regulator may have a depth of access in its observation of batches that includes or does not include specific data objects. The WorldREG super-regulator has almost equivalent permissions to the other regulators, except its query transaction does not extend down to KMP visibility. This distinction shows how regulators further up in the regulatory hierarchy do not necessarily need to have the greatest authority.

One simplification in SLAFKA of the original SLUMBAT Framework was removing the transporter-type holder. This highlights a subtlety regarding the purpose of the SLAFKA prototype, which was to perform material accounting by providing a clear history of discrete transactions—which was achieved—but not necessarily to provide real-time tracking of location or ownership of nuclear material in a way that goes beyond the detail of information currently reported for nuclear material accounting.

The content of this section has illustrated the type of discussions which took place between researchers and end users during the development of SLUMBAT, and SLAFKA, using terms of jurisdiction and role within the emerging overall idea of a framework for mapping a nuclear regulatory ecosystem to participant permissions in a DLT system. Initially developed for SLUMBAT, this SLUMBAT Framework [4] for nuclear material accounting and reporting on a permissioned blockchain was applied for a second time in the SLAFKA prototype.

The SLUMBAT Framework is transferable to other States, other areas of nuclear safeguards and, potentially, other nuclear regulatory structures, such as nuclear source licensing or nuclear security, which may follow the initial work on DLT for nuclear safeguards.

6 Reflections on SLUMBAT and SLAFKA

A conventional regulatory structure may be described in terms of level of authority and lines of reporting between participants. Operating organizations who hold nuclear material report upwards to their national regulator, who in turn reports upwards to a regional or international authority. This is how NUMBAT and SAFKA work. The authority over data increases towards the upper levels because participants with increased responsibility/oversight obtain de-facto read and write authority in their role in preserving data that originates from all participants 'below' them in this hierarchy.

In workshops involving the SLUMBAT and SLAFKA demos described here, it is anecdotally observed that interacting with the DLT materials accounting systems changes the dynamic between users, compared to a hierarchical system. In a DLT system all participants, operators, and regulators alike, interact on a more equal level with the blockchain, which itself becomes a separate entity that is authoritative for all parties. However, this does rely to a significant extent on trust in the protection of confidential data that would be shared with other peers, and it remains to be seen how placing real safeguards data on peer nodes could affect the group dynamic.

SLUMBAT and SLAFKA were not designed to meet any specific standards for information security and, beyond its ability to deliver user stories, the development process did not place any constraints around the operation of the DLT back end. While DLT can in principle achieve the level of security required, the current method used in SLAFKA of enforcing the access controls through chaincode alone is likely insufficient to provide the security needed for storing real nuclear safeguards data. This approach remains vulnerable to potential logical errors in smart contacts [17] and therefore formal verification of functional properties of the smart contracts [18] would be required for a future SLAFKA to be accepted as a production version.

Another known vulnerability exists in the execution of the query function, which currently reads blockchain records into computer memory before separating out records which relate to the user who is requesting the query.

In SLAFKA, the arrangement of web server and GUI is another potential vulnerability to information security, because the web server acts as a single point of influence between all the peer nodes and instances of the GUIs that their users interact with. Thus, the web server has a very high level of control over all transactions, to the extent that, if compromised, it could easily spoof user interactions and send direct instructions to the peer nodes without actual user consent.

Assuming DLT developments can offer the required level of confidence in the security of shared data, the SLUMBAT Framework has the potential to encode legislation and streamline reporting between stakeholders in complex regulatory ecosystems. The nuclear regulatory regime offers multiple examples of where this would be desirable, e.g. where a radioactive source may be regulated by both a federal and regional safety regulator, a federal safeguards regulator, and be subject to import rules imposed by customs agencies. SLAFKA has demonstrated how data entered in a DLT system by a nuclear operator can be made available almost simultaneously to three different regulators, with potential for different levels of oversight by each one.

Ongoing discussion [19] questions whether DLT represents an implicit threat to conventional regulatory structures, such as the IAEA, because many of its initial proponents strongly advocated DLT as a means for disintermediation. However, the relationship between DLT and decentralization is not simple and linear (as in, more DLT means more decentralization) because it depends on what aspect of the regulatory system is being decentralized. Decentralization may refer to [20] architectural decentralization, meaning the number and separation of physical computers involved in the provision of the network; political decentralization, in the numbers of individuals and organizations who control the computers in the network; and logical decentralization—the homogeneity of the logical and data structures used in different parts of the network.

In terms of these three dimensions, moving nuclear material accounting to a DLT system broadly implies increasing architectural and political decentralization, as more organizations and facilities become involved in providing the network, and potentially in validating the data stored on the network. This clearly has benefits in information resilience as data exists in multiple copies, and potentially also in increasing trust—if security concerns can be addressed, and if participants agree on access controls and requisite endorsement protocols.

However increased DLT adoption would likely rely on increased standardization, e.g., more logical centralization of reporting standards. In addition, nuclear safeguards are already implemented in a comprehensive policy ecosystem, to which any information management systems would seem to be subservient, being regulated ultimately by organizations that respond to changes in policy guidance.

Researchers building SLUMBAT and SLAFKA experienced the wide design flexibility of information systems based on DLT, where most design choices are not regulated by constraints in the software, but rather by the software developer's ability to elicit and correctly deliver user requirements. DLT in many ways feels like a natural fit to existing safeguards information management systems. If user requirements are sourced from a representative range of stakeholders and legislation advances in tandem with technology, the disruption to existing systems seems manageable.

7 Future Development of DLT for Nuclear Safeguards

One area where further advance of DLT for nuclear safeguards needs more research is the definition of the endorsement polices for future nuclear material accounting systems. The customization of endorsement policies presents a wide range of choices for the operation of future SLAFKA-like prototypes in terms of political and architectural decentralization—ranging from the almost completely centralized versions where all verification and subsequent data storage takes place centrally at the national regulator, to highly distributed versions with all national peers and potentially even international partners storing copies of the ledger and contributing to the verification of transactions. It should be emphasized that DLT does not mandate either extreme, rather offers the opportunity to choose an optimal solution along this continuum.

Decisions about the type of information being stored also remain to be made. SLAFKA stored all batch information at all nodes, but there are also likely to be benefits, from an information security standpoint, in storing partial batch information, encrypted or partially encrypted batch information, or cryptographic hashes of batch information in the peer nodes. For Hyperledger Fabric, use of channels would be integral in the implementation of such policies. If the solution were to require storing large auxiliary files for nuclear safeguards, such as multimedia files, an additional peer-to-peer data storage layer would become necessary, for example InterPlanetary File System (IPFS). As the SLUMBAT Framework demonstrates, such design choices can be specific to the type of information and the identity of the peer.

While a production-ready system for DLT nuclear material accounting remains yet to be attempted, the prototypes described here have validated the basic applicability and feasibility of this use case. Using an incremental and iterative approach to software development, and with the help of international partners, the UNSW researchers followed the application of DLT in safeguards from modest beginnings to an international prototype in two years. Further research on the application of DLT for nuclear safeguards will advance the development of working prototypes, like SLUMBAT and SLAFKA, to simultaneously demonstrate possible advantages of this approach to safeguards information management, while also serving as an engagement tool to elicit feedback on remaining unknowns in the user requirements.

References

1. International Atomic Energy Agency (2017) MOSAIC: the modernization of safeguards information technology. Available at: https://www.iaea.org/sites/default/files/17/01/mosaic.pdf. Accessed 10 June 2020
2. Everton C, Stohr R (2018) NUMBAT: lessons learned from Australia's database development. Paper presented at the symposium on international safeguards: building future safeguards capabilities. International Atomic Energy Agency, Vienna, 5–8 November 2018
3. Yu E, Obbard EG, Le L (2018) Evaluation of a blockchain based nuclear materials accounting platform in Australia. Paper presented at the symposium on international safeguards: building

future safeguards capabilities. International Atomic Energy Agency, Vienna, 5–8 November 2018. https://doi.org/10.26190/yb65-9476

4. Yu E et al (2021) The SLUMBAT demo of blockchain based nuclear safeguards. J Nucl Sci Technol 58(6):725–733. https://doi.org/10.1080/00223131.2020.1858990

5. Vestergaard C et al (2020) SLAFKA: Demonstrating the potential for distributed ledger technology for nuclear safeguards information management. Stimson Center, Washington, D.C. https://doi.org/10.13140/RG.2.2.32961.17764. Available at: https://www.stimson.org/2020/slafka/. Accessed 10 June 2021

6. International Atomic Energy Agency (2014) International safeguards in the design of nuclear reactors. Nuclear Energy Series No. NP-T-2.9, IAEA, Vienna, and: International Atomic Energy Agency (1999) Design measures to facilitate implementation of safeguards at future water cooled nuclear power plants, Technical Reports Series No. 392. IAEA, Vienna

7. The Linux Foundation (2020) What is kubernetes? Available at: https://kubernetes.io/docs/concepts/overview/what-is-kubernetes/. Accessed 27 May 2021

8. Cohn M (2004) User stories applied: for Agile software development. Addison-Wesley Professional

9. Frazar S et al (2019) Evaluating member state acceptance of blockchain for nuclear safeguards. Stanley Center for Peace and Security, Muscatine, Iowa

10. International Atomic Energy Agency (2016) Safeguards implementation practices guide on provision of information to the IAEA. IAEA-SVS-33. IAEA, Vienna

11. Androulaki E et al (2018) Hyperledger Fabric: a distributed operating system for permissioned blockchains. Paper presented at proceedings of the thirteenth EuroSys conference. ACM (EuroSys '18), New York, NY, USA, 23–26 April 2018, pp 30:1–30:15

12. Euratom, (2005) Commission regulation (Euratom) No 302/2005. Official J Eur Union 48(L54):1–70

13. International Atomic Energy Agency (2017) Subsidiary arrangement code 10: contents, format and structure of reports to the agency. SG-FM-1172. Available at: https://www.iaea.org/sites/default/files/sg-fm-1170-subsidiary-arrangement-code-10-labelled.pdf. Accessed 10 June 2021

14. Cisar V et al (2008) Nuclear material accounting handbook. International Atomic Energy Agency (IAEA Services Series No. 15)

15. Frazar A et al. (2019) Transit matching blockchain prototype. Pacific Northwest National Laboratory

16. International Atomic Energy Agency (1972) The structure and content of agreements between the agency and states required in connection with the treaty on the non-proliferation of nuclear weapons, *INFCIRC/153*. IAEA, Vienna

17. Khan ZA, Namin AS (2020) A survey on vulnerabilities of Ethereum smart contracts. arXiv [cs.CR]. Available at: http://arxiv.org/abs/2012.14481. Accessed 27 May 2021

18. Beckert B et al. (2018) Formal specification and verification of Hyperledger Fabric chaincode. Paper presented at the 3rd symposium on distributed ledger technology (SDLT-2018) co-located with ICFEM 2018: the 20th international conference on formal engineering methods. Gold Coast, Australia, 12 Nov 2018, pp 44–48

19. Frazar S (2021) Blockchain applications for Nuclear Safeguards. In: Vestergaard C (ed) Blockchain for international security. Springer Publishing

20. Buterin V (2017) The meaning of decentralization. Medium. Available at: https://medium.com/@VitalikButerin/the-meaning-of-decentralization-a0c92b76a274. Accessed 27 May 2021

Possibilities of Blockchain Technology for Nuclear Security

Maria Lovely Umayam

Abstract This chapter summarizes key concepts and stakeholders involved in implementing and maintaining strong security to protect nuclear materials and facilities. It then considers potential blockchain use-cases for the nuclear sector that could build confidence and trust among various stakeholders by tracking and securing data. It also lists criteria necessary for blockchain to be accepted and adopted by the nuclear enterprise.

1 Introduction

Along with nuclear safeguards, developing measures to protect nuclear material, including radioactive sources, from non-state adversaries is a critical facet of national security planning.[1] Failure to do so can lead to grave consequences: the theft, sabotage, or unauthorized transfer and use of these highly sensitive and dangerous materials [1]. While nuclear security is considered as part of national policy for countries with well-established nuclear sectors, the concept was largely unacknowledged and under prioritized until 2001, when the September 11 terrorist attack on the United States forced governments around the world to rethink their security responses to all types of terrorist threats and consider overlooked vulnerabilities in systems that were otherwise thought secure [2].

---

[1] For the purposes of this chapter, nuclear security also includes the protection of radioactive sources, which are used for various scientific, medical, and industrial applications. While nuclear materials and radioactive sources have different characteristics, stakeholders, threat profiles, and security considerations, they both share the need for streamlined and secure information flows and communication channels to prevent adversaries from exploiting these materials. For simplicity, the chapter will focus on processes and stakeholders often associated with nuclear materials.

M. L. Umayam (✉)
45 1/2 Westminster Ave, Venice, CA 90291, USA
e-mail: lovely@bombshelltoe.com

The Henry L. Stimson Center, Washington, DC, USA

© Springer Nature Switzerland AG 2021   55
C. Vestergaard (ed.), *Blockchain for International Security*,
Advanced Sciences and Technologies for Security Applications,
https://doi.org/10.1007/978-3-030-86240-4_5

Since then, countries have moved quickly to evaluate the security of major business sectors handling sensitive assets and activities, such as critical infrastructure. For the nuclear sector, many experts raised concerns about terrorist organizations' (namely al Qaeda) open intentions to obtain nuclear materials and expertise, as well as some facilities' outdated security frameworks that render them vulnerable terrorist targets [3]. The spotlight on nuclear security brightened in 2010 when more than 50 world leaders agreed to participate in the first Nuclear Security Summit held in Washington, DC (this was followed by meetings every two years until 2016) with the purpose of creating an informal international forum that openly encouraged collective norm-building around the protection of nuclear material [4]. Even with the increasing attention and progressive approaches on nuclear security, challenges remain: how do countries keep these materials secure when the face of the threat is constantly changing? Can new technologies help?

Although there has yet to be an international terrorist attack to rival the loss incurred during September 11, countries must continuously improve their means of identifying and assessing risk and adapting their security measures accordingly. To be proactive can be hard to practice: since it is difficult to anticipate future threats, it is challenging to gauge the risks involved and plan an effective security response [5]. Layering redundant security measures do not guarantee better outcomes if the risks cannot be properly identified against the changing nature of the threat: e.g., a cyber threat instead of a physical one, or perhaps a mix of both [6]. Applied to the nuclear sector, the common (and readily accepted) recommendation to apply more security by increasing back-up forces only yields incremental improvements [7]. In particular, some experts worry that overcompensating would be counterproductive since making sophisticated, tightly coupled systems even more intricate becomes its own form of vulnerability [8]. Even in a post-September 11 environment, nuclear security measures have not been demonstrably sufficient: in 2019, 189 unauthorized activities involving nuclear materials and radioactive sources (including incidents of trafficking and malicious use) were reported by 36 countries to the International Atomic Energy Agency (IAEA) [9]. The IAEA also observed another revealing trend of a steady number of reported unauthorized activities and events since 2003 [9]. While these incidents are not directly linked to malicious use, it still indicates deficiencies in nuclear security regimes, holes that allow materials to slip out of regulatory control—unwittingly or not.

Two decades after September 11, the security landscape for nuclear facilities is even more complex with the increase of cyber-related threats. Many industries servicing critical infrastructures worry about the increased cyberattack vectors targeting operational technologies. From a recent survey of about 1,700 utility professionals, 56% reported operational loss, and about 25% shared that they have experienced "mega attacks" with more sophisticated means of finding vulnerabilities [10]. The nuclear sector has seen its fair share of cyberattacks in the past four years, with nuclear operators finding hackers attempting to study computer networks in facilities potentially to plan a far larger, more devastating attack in the future [11, 12]. Moreover, large-scale disasters such as the Covid-19 pandemic exposed the frailty of the current world order. Governments saw the ways in which long-standing systems—supply chains, financial institutions, health agencies—were slow to react and adapt during a crisis. According to the cyber security research group Check Point Research, 71% of surveyed security professionals reported an increase in security attacks since the Covid-19 outbreak [13]. A hit on critical infrastructures can be devastating; the May 2021 Colonial Pipeline incident, a ransomware attack (hackers stealing and withholding data via encryption and releasing it unless ransom is paid) on a major American fuel pipeline forced redistribution of diesel and gas across the country, and triggered concerns of supply scarcity [14].

Therein lies the crux of nuclear security challenge: how do countries keep highly sensitive and dangerous materials secure when the face of the threat is changing, sometimes in unprecedented ways? What types of security measures or approaches can prevail amidst these global shifts? The use of "breakthrough" technologies like Distributed Ledger Technology (DLT) could help illuminate potential answers to these questions. While research on the use of DLT to improve security in nuclear facilities is still in its nascent stages, government and industry stakeholders have already shown enthusiasm to test possibilities. Application of DLT within the nuclear field has been recently explored in top-level conversations in the United Nations and the IAEA, and in some cases, the technology is being prototyped by government and non-government entities in select countries [15, 16].

A potentially applicable aspect of DLT, which will be explored further in this chapter, is to provide data integrity across communication systems, which in turn creates an environment of accountability and governance among information managers and users. The notion of trust in the context of security (especially cyber security) is incredibly complicated, given that the standard approach is to trust nothing and verify everything [17]. It will be important to study and critique how DLT supports this idea of security, especially the possibility of developing an unchangeable ledger of information that could show managers and/or users data origin and access points, including when, where, and by whom certain information within the network was shared, changed, or accessed. For nuclear security, the ability to trace data in this manner could make it inherently difficult for adversaries to manipulate facility or material-relevant data to cover any nefarious activities (deter), enhance nuclear material surveillance and personnel monitoring (detect), and help relevant authorities to immediately ascertain patterns in activity/decision-making (response).

More radically, exploring the application of DLT for nuclear security could expand the ways in which the nuclear field conceptualizes the very notion of security. Instead of establishing a physical perimeter or barrier to protect an object (what physical protection already accomplishes), DLT platforms are suited towards tracking and authenticating information flows: chain of custody, access, movement, and interactions that could occur inside or outside nuclear facilities. As more organizations and companies adopt DLT systems to help track and verify data, it is worth observing how, if at all, it can complement existing physical protection measures.

The following sections discuss the role of security within the larger nuclear enterprise; the key players responsible for creating and maintaining nuclear security regimes; the challenges that influence the current security landscape and engender distrust among these stakeholders; and what a DLT platform could possibly provide to enhance existing nuclear security approaches, as well as barriers and other challenges to overcome.

2 The Basics of Nuclear Security—Objectives and Principles

Nuclear security is one critical piece in the global agenda to prevent the spread of nuclear weapons and is specifically dedicated to the protection of nuclear and radiological material, as well as associated facilities against the malicious intent of state and non-state actors. While nuclear security has this unique mandate, it coexists with other elements that bolster the rest of the nuclear nonproliferation regime. Nuclear safeguards, which is discussed in the previous two chapters, is a discipline that is separate but intertwined with nuclear security. Although safeguards—the technical verification of nuclear material to ensure governments are only using them for peaceful purposes—is geared towards state compliance, some of its methods and approaches can be harmonized with security objectives. A nuclear material accountancy system, which entails proficiency in maintaining precise knowledge about nuclear material quantity, location, and other important characteristics, is a crucial component of safeguards reporting. And if done effectively, a material accountancy system can also be a tool to detect any foul play (e.g., unauthorized removal of nuclear material or insider threats) in a timely manner which lends itself to strong security [18].

Another concept inextricably linked with nuclear security is safety: maintaining the proper conditions in nuclear facilities to prevent unintended accidents (i.e., radioactive hazards) that can cause undue harm to frontline workers, the environment, and the greater public [19]. The objectives of safety and security are different, but they share common threads: both require an assessment of respective risks, prioritize early prevention and detection, and ultimately champion the protection of society and the environment [21]. For example, an operator might decide to erect a strong protective barrier around a nuclear facility that can serve the purpose of safety (contain radiological release) and security (defend the perimeter). But these two concepts can also clash. Some of the core principles of security (limiting access to certain areas) may run contrary to the values of safety (the need for a quick and clear exit). In considering the application of breakthrough technologies like DLT to strengthen security, it is important to understand the ways in which it may interface and impact other disciplines such as safeguards, safety, and security. Ideally, a DLT platform would enhance the complementarity of all three, or at least would not inadvertently obstruct each other's goals.

Protecting nuclear materials and facilities is not technology-driven, but human-dependent. Notable nuclear security incidents, including the successful breach of the Y-12 National Security Complex in the United States by a group of protestors, as well as the more recent revelation that Japan's Tepco-owned Kashiwazaki-Kariwa nuclear power plant suffers from severe security vulnerabilities, largely stem from human negligence or error. Investigators of the 2012 Y-12 incident found that while the security alarms detected intruders in the facility premises, security officers failed to promptly investigate the situation, believing that it was another false alarm [20]. In the Japan case, officials found that facility staffers used other employee ID cards to gain access around the grounds [21]. Both instances illustrate the ways physical and information security can easily crumble without the right security mindset within the workforce. Security experts warn that too much technology—whether it becomes too overwhelming and complex to manage, or too automated that it encourages a complacent attitude—can degrade security infrastructure and culture of an organization [22]. As such, it will be important to consider how a DLT platform, irrespective of the new technological benefits it presents, could potentially negatively impact security values and attitudes.

As a discipline, nuclear security manifests at the international, national, and operational levels. The amended Convention for the Physical Protection of Nuclear Material (A/CPPNM) that entered into force in 2016 is the only legally binding international treaty that requires countries to implement physical protection measures for nuclear materials in nuclear facilities, as well as in transport [23]. The A/CCPNM also obligates states to establish punitive measures for individuals or organizations engaged in unauthorized or illegal activity with nuclear material. The amended Convention also makes clear that while nuclear security requires international coordination and commitment, it is still the sole responsibility of the state to establish and implement a nuclear security regime with strong physical protection [24]. Indeed, the face of the threat may be different depending on a given country's nuclear capabilities (and hence, the types of materials it holds), as well as geopolitical standing that may or may not make it a target. Unlike for safeguards reporting, the IAEA does not track and verify country compliance for nuclear security. The IAEA does offer recommendations on how countries may choose to develop their respective security regimes and could offer assistance by way of trainings or International Physical Protection Advisory Service (IPPAS) missions, should countries request it.

The A/CPPNM includes twelve fundamental principles that should be embodied in each country's nuclear security regime. While broad, these principles serve as a guiding template to ensure that all countries understand the key characteristics that make a nuclear security regime effective. All twelve fundamental principles offer valuable insights to a strong security regime, but there are three that are particularly notable considering DLT's authentication and traceability characteristics:

- Security Culture (Fundamental Principle F) highlights the need for all facility personnel—from senior executives to the frontline workers—to believe in the credibility of a security threat and possess the right values to uphold vigilance and commitment to security. Since culture is difficult to quantify and may vary depending on country and facility, many nuclear facility operators lament the inherent challenges of diagnosing and sharing culture-specific problems. Technical and security experts are currently studying how to pair blockchain with existing access controls to create a tamper-proof access control management system into physical spaces [25]. If DLT can be used to improve existing controls and strengthen gatekeeping for specific sensitive locations, it can potentially eliminate human error, including the accidental sharing of access, or worse, an intentional infiltration by an insider threat.

- Defense in Depth (Fundamental Principle I) advises countries to develop physical protection plans that include an appropriate combination of facility design (gates); procedures (reliable performance of guards and other personnel); and computer security (hardware and software). Defense in depth requires strategic decisions to design security arrangements in a way that cannot be anticipated by an adversary, delaying their plans. DLT, especially if paired with Internet of Things (IoT) sensors that monitor real-time conditions, could provide added information transparency, such that the appropriate nuclear security stakeholders are always equipped with trustworthy data about the when/where/what (e.g., the location, movement, and storage of nuclear material within their facilities and borders) of nuclear material. This DLT-IoT technology is already being implemented to monitor temperature-sensitive medicines such as vaccines as it travels along the supply chain. The use of a DLT platform helps log and match designated shipment locations of vaccines in transit; officials are then notified of potential diversion (vaccine theft, accidental detours, and spoilage has always been a logistical issue worldwide) [26, 27]. A similar use-case could enhance detection of material diversion when layers of defense in depth are breached in real-time.

- Confidentiality (Fundamental Principle L) emphasizes the need for countries to protect sensitive information such that only those designated with a certain level of trustworthiness are given access. To achieve this, nuclear facilities should specify what types of information should be protected (i.e., business operations vs. nuclear material information), how it should be protected, and who is privy to this information. Nuclear security practitioners are inclined to restrict all flows of information to diminish the likelihood of leaks or other unwanted transfers of data. While overcompensating for security by way of confidentiality is generally positive, there are also real trade-offs: it could inadvertently curtail appropriate information sharing among operators or countries for the greater benefit of the nuclear security community. Today, technology experts are intrigued by DLT's process of cryptographically storing and linking data to a series of "blocks" using a hashing process, such that a block of data cannot be easily compromised since any changes made to it will make it incompatible with the rest of the chain. Companies like Blockcert are using DLT to create digital credentials such as diplomas and property deeds that can be shared and verified anywhere in the world [28]. It would be interesting to study how DLT could impact, if at all, credentialing of "need-to-know" personnel, thereby changing the way organizations and companies assign and ensure confidentiality.

The use of DLT to manage certain types of security-related data—not storing the sensitive/confidential information itself onto the blockchain, but the valuable metadata such as personnel access activities associated with certain information;

the status of nuclear material in transit; etc.—could significantly impact the ways countries implement the principles listed above. For instance, if metadata can be monitored and verified through a private or permissioned DLT platform (i.e., available to employee and senior management responsible for security supervision, and other coordinating outside entities that need to be in-the-know), this could help ascertain that security best practices are being taken seriously within the workforce.

DLT could also impact the ways countries approach physical security. Security measures that are fixed and structural in nature rely on a perimeter-centric approach to security—building defenses around an asset, in this case nuclear material. As mentioned above, technologists envision pairing DLT with Internet of Things (IoT)—devices that can be paired using the Internet such that they can "communicate" data across each other—for continuous monitoring of environments and conditions for security purposes. This would entail placing an IoT device on the asset itself, which would enable a passive data stream about the asset's status to feed directly into the chain [29]. While this might not be possible for several years, the implications are intriguing; this type of security strategy does not defend at the perimeter, but rather embeds onto the asset itself, so that it can assess and respond to the outside world. Seriously considering DLT for nuclear security demands an understanding of how it would impact the existing structures and communities that uphold them.

3 Trust Within the Nuclear Security Community

As the A/CPPNM affirms, countries are exclusively responsible for determining the parameters of their own nuclear security regimes given the unique threat profiles they face. Thus, nuclear security is implemented and enforced by a cast of characters at the national level, tasked to coordinate and hold each other accountable with their respective roles in upholding the security regime. But doing so comes with its own set of unique challenges:

Government bodies are responsible for developing the requisite laws and regulations that serve as the bedrock of a national security regime. The competent authority has direct authority to comprehensively assess the nature of the threat facing nuclear facilities in the country and materials in transit, based on most recent intelligence information. The threat assessment is often developed into a *Design Basis Threat*, which sets the limits to which nuclear operators must defend against the threat. Government entities can also immediately communicate to relevant stakeholders—including neighboring countries that may be affected—if a security incident is imminent or underway, which requires a nationally-coordinated response [30].

Challenge: Commitment to nuclear security can vary depending on national priorities. Some countries, like the United States, strongly advocate for nuclear security because counterterrorism is more urgent in their agendas. But for others, nuclear security may not be at the forefront of national priorities since the threat is not as immediately recognized, or that the consequences are deemed acceptable. Moreover, effective security is largely invisible; it is harder to advocate for security when its successes are not easily tangible. This could make information sharing on nuclear security disjointed as some countries emphasize it more than others.

Competent authorities are established to enact national law and oversee the implementation of regulations. To do their jobs effectively, competent authorities have a clearly defined legal mandate to verify that nuclear facilities maintain compliance with security measures that would adequately respond to the requirements under the Design Basis Threat. Therefore, the competent authority should evaluate adherence to security regulations (sometimes by way of inspections); have access to nuclear material accounting information; and have immediate knowledge to any nuclear security incidents/events.

Challenge: Since the robustness of competent authorities are dictated by the laws and regulations passed by their respective governments, their capacity could be constrained due to political or economic reasons. In some cases, competent authorities exist but do not have the requisite legal enforcement—the "teeth" to compel stakeholders to follow orders—to assert certain security standards.

License Holders (nuclear facility operators/shippers) are at the forefront of the nuclear security regime, accountable for implementing security requirements that meet the Design Basis Threat and reported to the competent authority. To conduct their business, they must apply for a license, which requires demonstrating their accountability in handling nuclear material, including a proper security plan at all times. Aside from regulations, license holders also conduct their own internal risk assessments to determine security factors into their entire business enterprise, and impact other risk considerations (financial, operational, and other risks).

Challenge: For license holders, security considerations cannot exist in a vacuum; it must be based on a risk-informed approach, while balanced with other operational demands to run a sustainable business. Operators often cite rising costs as a challenge to security implementation since maintaining a combination of effective measures to achieve strong defense-in-depth may be perceived too expensive in the long-run. This is tied to a larger challenge with respect to organizational *culture*—it is important for decision-makers in nuclear facilities to believe that the threat is real to take security (including investments towards it) seriously. Some experts worry that the current approach is primarily driven by meeting check-list requirements, instead of a true workplace alertness. In terms of information security, this could manifest as lack of mindfulness in the ways information is being communicated especially if stakeholders use different channels (hardcopy or electronic), and data being unwittingly or intentionally altered after the fact. These concerns are not unfounded; high-profile nuclear cyber security incidents like the 2003 Davis-Besse incident in the United States and the 2016 Gundremmingen incident in Germany trace the root-cause back to the most basic security violations of not updating computer patches or using prohibited portable devices [31, 32].

Overall, a robust nuclear security regime hinges on (1) effective implementation of nuclear security plans at the license holder-level to detect, delay, and respond to security incidents; and (2) immediate communication between license holders, competent authorities, government bodies when foul play is discovered or if a security incident occurs. *Timeliness* becomes a critical factor as these stakeholders interact.

License holders must be able to assess risk and detect vulnerabilities in a timely manner, as well as alert the competent authority should something go wrong. While seemingly straightforward, there are factors that could make this difficult.

A direct technological solution may not exist to overcome the challenges these different actors face, and at this stage of research, it is still too early to suggest that DLT is definitely applicable. However, it might be useful to study how DLT could provide relief in some areas. Working on nuclear security entails accessing sensitive information that could expose vulnerabilities in each country's infrastructure. Such a working environment where one is required to protect information at all cost can make it difficult to easily share information (and in some cases, believe information if there is fear of being misled). If a bridge of trust can be built through data such that all actors involved can agree to what types of security-relevant information can be shared with confidence under a DLT-backed environment, it could become the acceptable conduit for security stakeholders to communicate their concerns [33]. This allows for greater governance and would consequently yield improved and faster response to the threat. Framed this way, DLT for nuclear security is not about replacing existing physical protection measures (the guns, guards, and gates), but rather *complementing* it such that stakeholders have better knowledge about the performance and behaviors of their guards; the conditions of their gates; and whether the guns are ready to respond in the event of a security breach.

4 Potential Pathways for DLT

The use of DLT systems to strengthen nuclear security is still at the beginning stages [34]. More research is necessary to arrive at the best use-case scenario that can clearly articulate the specific security challenge it is addressing (what is it helping deter/detect/delay/respond to) and whether relevant stakeholders agree that it is:

- *Feasible*: Do the technology and financial resources exist to pursue a use-case?
- *Reliable*: Will the technology yield consistent and trustworthy information to help determine security-related decisions among the stakeholders outlined above?
- *Desirable*: Would license holders and regulators readily integrate this with existing systems and processes, or does this technology demonstrate a clear advantage than what is already being used?
- *Sustainable*: Is this technology going to last fifteen or twenty years from now or is this a short-lived "hype"?

DLT's enhanced capacity to address cyber-related challenges has drawn increased interest in various sectors, and the nuclear community would benefit from following their trials closely. After surveying the security benefits in healthcare and finance—the two groups that readily adopted blockchain for information management and security—researchers found that companies are particularly pleased with DLT's alternative model to traditional centralized security systems [35]. Centralized systems are especially vulnerable to external attacks since it aggregates sensitive information and decision-making to a single point of failure. DLT can employ a combination of features including hashing (used the hash function stored on the blockchain, which can be used to verify that the data they received matches the original by running it through the same hashing algorithm and comparing results); segregating node clusters (only certain individuals have access to certain types of information within a chain); and immutable, irreversible ledger system (every activity is logged to allow a robust track record)—a novel de-centralized approach to data management where users do not necessarily have to depend on a middle-man to implement information security. If an attack occurs, an adversary will face a herculean encryption challenge to cover up their tracks, and parts of the system could be easily salvaged since data management architecture is evenly distributed.

DLT's security model is already in action for electronic medical records: *MedRec*, a DLT health data management platform developed by MIT, does not store sensitive patient information, but places a *signature* of the record on a private blockchain that the patients themselves are able to manage and verify that it has not been passed on to other people without their consent [36]. *MedRec* introduces data ownership and governance to patients, which ultimately spreads security measures beyond a centralized institution to the specific stakeholders (in this case, patients) that have a vested interest in the integrity of their medical record system.

However, it is important to note that if adopted to nuclear security, stakeholders must not lose sight of its purpose: a complement, not a substitute, for existing physical protection measures. It serves to organize, analyze, and transmit information to those deemed need-to-know such that the security plan for a given organization or facility can be implemented with a greater sense of confidence. As the nuclear field deliberates potential pathways leading to the use of DLT for security purposes, it may be helpful to consider these questions along the way:

Is it risk-informed? Different types of nuclear material have varying levels of risk depending on factors such as quantity, type (element, isotope, irradiation), and form (physical or chemical). Per IAEA recommendations and international consensus on nuclear material categorization for security purposes, nuclear material typically fall under Category I, II, III. Category I material is considered the most sensitive and "attractive" to foul play, hence additional security measures are required. Category II, III have lower "attractive" features respectively, which demand commensurate security details. For example, proper security for Category I material entail storage in an additional inner/vital area in a protected area, while Category II should be stored in a protected area, and Category III material in a limited area. Varying degrees of intrusion detection instruments and response forces apply depending on the category. Thus, a DLT platform must be developed in such a way that understands which types of nuclear material require higher levels of protection given the risks they carry. This may be relevant if DLT is used to track employee access to certain types of material—it is best practice for facilities to keep records of all personnel who direct or indirect access to inner/vital areas housing Category I material. Perhaps signatures of records of personnel access or activity in inner/vital areas could be stored on the chain, since this is already a requirement for Category I material.

Can it provide timely information? As emphasized above, nuclear security heavily relies on timely detection of intrusion. As stated on IAEA recommendations, license holders (nuclear facility operators) must have the capability to conduct an emergency inventory check as soon as possible within the time-period specified by the country [37]. Integrating a DLT platform with an eye towards assisting security should consider whether it lends additional timeliness that would help license holders ascertain discrepancies in the data much faster.

What type of information will be logged and who will be given access? Security decisions are made based on reliable sensitive information only privy to select personnel in a facility, as well as the corresponding competent authorities tasked to keep the nuclear sector accountable. Depending on the facility's classification scheme (again, following a risk-informed approach in accordance with national law/regulations), information about nuclear material is digitally secured, communicated through code or manually delivered accompanied by certified personnel. If a DLT platform is used, it is critical to evaluate what types of information stakeholders are willing to place on the blockchain, and which nodes would be trusted to allow access and perform verification processes for the rest of the network. All stakeholders involved must feel confident in using DLT as a platform, or else risk fracturing the trust required to carry out security-related work.

5 Promising Use Case: Transport Security

Transport security is one of the most complex security challenges in the nuclear sector due to its dynamic nature. First, there is the issue of scale: according to the latest figures, about 20 million shipments of nuclear material and radioactive sources—varying in quantities and types—transit throughout the world every year whether by air, sea, or road (sometimes a combination if it is an international shipment) [38]. If the nuclear sector continues to grow—may it be through next-generation power reactors or continued reliance on nuclear R&D—transport is also expected to expand as a business. For instance, experts estimate a rise in the transport of spent nuclear fuel due to worldwide reclamation projects and the growing interest in fuel "take-back" agreements for nonproliferation purposes [39, 40].

Transportation also grapples with changing jurisdictions as the cargo moves great distances and crosses borders. When nuclear material travels across countries, security responsibility transitions between governments that may have different prioritizations and requirements for their respective nuclear security regimes. This introduces an organizational complication if a security incident occurs and is not properly communicated due to a lag in notice or response between governments. Tracking movement is the second complicating factor unique for this sector. The fluidity of the environment not only requires a clear understanding of chain of custody, but also introduces uncontrollable variables that may not fit the security plan. For example, a delay in receiving nuclear material due to unforeseen but mundane circumstances (i.e., logistical mix-ups, delay in conveyance schedules, etc.) could open vulnerabilities not addressed in the plan. A famous incident in Mexico involving a high-jacked hospital truck (en route to a nuclear waste disposal site) holding dangerous radioactive material, unbeknownst to the perpetrators, illustrates that theft is a variable to be taken seriously, irrespective whether the target is sensitive material or not [41]. In this case, the lack of preparedness for such a scenario seriously compromised the material inside it, even if this was not the specific intent.

While not all transport companies handle such sensitive and highly dangerous assets, they confront the same problems when protecting their cargo in a dynamic environment, especially in demonstrating that the product was not compromised or touched by a questionable source as it makes its way from producer to recipient. As discussed elsewhere in this book, supply chain logistics management—including the transport of components or final products—benefit greatly from DLT technology due to its groundbreaking innovation for transaction management, allowing customer transparency into a typically opaque process. As more companies test DLT platforms for supply chain management (as seen by the most prominent venture to date, Tradelens, a blockchain demo between IBM and Maersk), the nuclear community is also beginning to see potential advantages for security. Tracing goods in a secure platform could allow certain stakeholders involved in product movement to "roadmap" their routes from origin to destination, especially in logging stops and exchange points where the product changes custody [42].

Supply chain DLT prototypes are also exploring how to blockchain certain credentials to help ease the verification process of documents involved in a shipment, e,g., bills of lading, manifests, licenses, certificates, etc [43]. From a security standpoint, verifying the authenticity of documents and stakeholders minimizes the potential for fraud. The London-based company Tracr combines DLT, IoT, artificial intelligence, and privacy/security technology to develop a single digital platform for recording diamond manufacturing and trade, with the goal of ensuring that the diamond is responsibly sourced and acquired from end-to-end [44]. DLT comes into play by establishing and "matching" two immutable ledgers as a diamond moves along the chain: (1) the digital asset such as e-documents, authorizations, and other information about a given diamond; (2) the material asset or the unique physical attributes of the diamond itself (i.e., etchings on the surface of the diamond that is scanned as part of its ID). This pairing of digital and material becomes the fixed record tracked throughout transit. Representatives from the trucking industry have shown support in experimenting with DLT as an underlying tracking technology for all types of products. For instance, the Blockchain in Transport Alliance (BiTA) has seen an exponential increase in membership queries from transport companies—they reported a surge of 900 application in 2018 alone—interested in understanding how DLT, especially if it achieves interoperability or "cross-chain" features, can better track freight effectively than the current process recording data using electronic data interchange (EDI) technology. Trucking companies are particularly interested in seeing how DLT, especially if it achieves interoperability or "cross-chain" features, can better track freight effectively than the current process recording data using electronic data interchange (EDI) technology [45].

Finally, there may be additional benefits to using a digital ledger, especially if stakeholders can agree to evaluate subsets of the data to learn from trends. The Insur-Wave platform, jointly developed by A.P Moller—Maersk, accounting firm EY, DLT developer Guardtime, and other industry stakeholders, presents an intriguing test case of what rigorous data collection through DLT could possibly offer. The Insur-Wave platform connects shippers, brokers, and insurers together to facilitate common transactions including tracking assets, negotiating premiums, and paying claims. By overlaying specific data elements gathered overtime, InsurWave can help identify risk exposure for shippers and insurers, i.e., choosing a certain shipping route already known for turbulent waters/piracy can increase the likelihood of risk compared to an established safer route. With this information readily available, industry hopes that it can make informed business decisions in real-time [46]. Ultimately, the goal is to create a transparent space for all these actors involved to conduct business and share information with the collective goal of minimizing business disruption. While nuclear operators observe special liability principles, the InsurWave model is nonetheless a thought-provoking project to strengthen industry-to-industry transparency for the sake of operational efficiency and data security.

Using these initial observations from supply chain management as a launching point, a potential DLT platform for nuclear transport security could include the following components:

Risk-informed approach: A DLT platform for nuclear security could organize and segregate information depending on nuclear material characterization or attractiveness being transported, since they pose different risks that must be addressed by the appropriate level of security measures/security plan. Thus, DLT developers must work with security experts to differentiate data architecture to cater to different categories.

Harmonizing digital and material assets: Similar to Tracr's paradigm, the DLT platform architecture for transport security ideally should accommodate and reconcile a digital information ledger (the information about the material being moved) and the physical material ledger (a unique identifier for the package or cask containing the nuclear material), as shown in Fig. 1. This way, the paper trail of a given shipment is always in lockstep with the physical material, especially if some form of

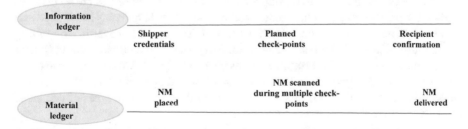

Fig. 1 Potential model of two blockchain ledgers storing digital information and data regarding physical movement of material

transfer occurs—operator to shipper, or in more complex scenarios, when it changes conveyance (plane to road) or when it crosses borders.

To conceptualize how these two ledgers interact while taking into account the different levels of risks to help facilitate secure transport, it may be helpful to think about the different transport scenarios where a DLT platform could apply.

Transport within facility: In large facilities, nuclear material might have to be transported between sites via in-house shuttles, especially during refueling. As noted above, nuclear material may be stored in a limited, protected, or vital/inner area depending on whether it is Category I, II, or III. It may be beneficial to log access points of personnel (e.g., entering or exiting; type of activity) that have permission to access these materials to verify that they followed proper protocols. Such information—perhaps metadata or the *hashes* of data (while the actual data remains "off-chain" in a separate database)—could be logged onto a potential blockchain platform. This information would only be accessible between the personnel and appropriate management (immediate supervisor, chief security officer, etc.), and should be integrated/compatible with existing procedures to monitor access to information and other insider threat mitigation practices.

Transport between facilities (in-country): If the nuclear material is transported between facilities in the same country (for instance, a combination of rail and road across the United States), a DLT platform may be useful in authenticating shipper and recipient credentials, as well as "road-mapping" checkpoints—logging planned or unplanned stops—along the way, especially if there is a change in conveyance. For instance, most supply chain companies implementing DLT have connected their separate Enterprise Resource Planning (ERP)/Supply Chain Management (SCM) technology through an application programming interface to enable real-time track and trace or provenance [47]. Using DLT minimizes the likelihood of tampering information and could provide *timely* information that existing techniques (code-talk, waiting for paperwork, etc.) does not readily make available. RFID or IoT devices may be included on the shipment (i.e., packages, drums, or casks) to help with monitoring. This type of geo-tracking does not necessarily require a constant stream of data to be logged on the chain. It could be timed such that it is activated or scanned when a checkpoint is reached, or when the nuclear material *changes* hands that must be verified by matching the exchange at the documentation-level, as well as the material-level. And if operators, shippers, and competent authorities are so inclined to explore possibilities, certain elements of the data on the ledger may be collated and analyzed to understand the integrity/reliability of different routes overtime (similarly to the InsurWave risk-analysis capability). Moreover, confidentiality could impact operational processes, since some materials may be designated to be documented and delivered via hardcopy only, while some can be stored or shared through encrypted electronic files. Facility operators must be mindful of how these types of decisions can affect internal and external communication.

Transport between countries: In addition to the features described above, a DLT platform could help streamline information-sharing at the license holder- and competent authority-level, when multiple stakeholders representing different countries (hence, different capabilities and requirements under their respective nuclear regimes) are involved. For example, verifying shipper credentials across countries may be easier if a subset of information can be securely accessed through a blockchain, as opposed to reconciling different procedures depending on country requirements (i.e., preference for paper-based/manual communication, etc.) This may also help when interacting with customs and other port personnel, especially as ports are moving towards their own digital platforms to review important documentation [48]. More complicated (and politically charged), but equally important is the possibility of using DLT to link competent authorities together in the event of a security incident to facilitate faster sharing of information. Under the amended CPPNM, countries should establish some form of communication channels especially among neighboring countries for this purpose. More research may be conducted to determine feasibility for incident reporting in this context.

6 Future Considerations

While DLT is slow to achieve mainstream adoption, it has gained interest in several industries to receive million-dollar investments to test its promising capabilities. In the supply chain sector, the Maersk and IBM-led blockchain projects such as Tradelens have gradually amassed a formidable membership including major global container carriers that would effectively place half the world's shipping data on the blockchain [49]. And as noted in the examples found throughout the book, businesses in the health, mineral, and energy sectors have shared demonstrable gains from streamlining and tracking their information through the blockchain. But examples related to highly sensitive, dangerous goods are not readily available. A test phase is critical—perhaps using fictional data as a start—to acquire buy-in. For the nuclear sector, the benefits will not be evident until a prototype is developed in conjunction with the appropriate stakeholders, so that they can observe first-hand DLT features that are *feasible,reliable,viable,and sustainable* for nuclear security. Without this critical step, DLT for nuclear security will remain a theoretical concept.

A critical challenge to overcome during a prototype is the instinctive skepticism security stakeholders will have to the idea of a "distributed" approach to security. In effect, DLT introduces a new paradigm that could potentially clash with the traditional system of centralizing information as a form of protection. It is expected (and understandable) that certain experts in the security field may misconstrue the notion of a "distributed" ledger as implying unfettered information sharing, degrading the current centralized model. Applied to the transport security use-case above, it may be a herculean task to convince governments to share sensitive information on a blockchain when existing channels of communication are already politically difficult. However, future advances in DLT technology such as interoperability—the ability to see and share across different sets of blockchains to facilitate agreements and transactions—could ease concerns if each stakeholder can control their own blockchain and set parameters that can be reported across chains. Overall, it will be very important to articulate—and ideally, demonstrate by way of a prototype—how DLT enhances the security of data management when data governance is spread amongst a strategic set of stakeholders to avoid a single-point of failure (i.e., a security incident that exposes information in the conventional, centralized database).

Since security is ultimately implemented by license holders, facility operators and shippers must have full understanding of the cost–benefit calculus of adapting DLT. Hence, a DLT prototype must be able to answer: how would this technology be a better solution than secure database tools readily available? Development and maintenance costs for DLT will vary depending on the scale (the number of nodes and transactions), as well as scope (what the technology attempts to achieve/risks it aims to minimize). The advantages must outweigh or overcome costs by either proving to be comparable to the costs of existing security measures, or showing a demonstrable additional advantage if costs are higher. As part of determining the scope and scale of DLT, the prototype must present a robust data acquisition strategy agreeable to all stakeholders involved. More specifically, it will be important for license holders to collectively identify what type of information is placed on the chain, or in other words, what information needs to be shared to other stakeholders in an immutable way. For the nuclear sector, certain metadata about nuclear material or facilities (i.e., signatures of personnel activity, material location in transit, etc.) that all stakeholders agree to share amongst each other in a secure manner may be an appropriate start. Overall, a prototype may reveal that DLT can offer its strengths in an overarching security strategy—a small but effective piece of a larger puzzle—instead of the one-stop solution.

References

1. International Atomic Energy Agency (2013) Objective and essential elements of a state's nuclear security regime. Nuclear Security Series 20. Available at: https://www-pub.iaea.org/MTCD/Publications/PDF/Pub1590_web.pdf. Accessed 25 May 2021
2. Bush GW (2002) State of the union address. Available at: https://georgewbush-whitehouse.arc hives.gov/news/releases/2002/01/20020129-11.html. Accessed 25 May 2021
3. Bunn M (2005) Preventing a nuclear 9/11. Available at: https://oconnell.fas.harvard.edu/files/matthew_bunn/files/bunn_preventing_a_nuclear_9-11.pdf. Accessed 25 May 2021; 9/11 Commission Report—Critical Infrastructure https://govinfo.library.unt.edu/911/report/911 Report.pdf. Accessed 25 May 2021
4. U.S. White House (2016) Fact sheet: the nuclear security summits—securing the world from terrorism. Available at: https://obamawhitehouse.archives.gov/the-press-office/2016/03/29/fact-sheet-nuclear-security-summits-securing-world-nuclear-terrorism. Accessed 25 May 2021
5. Comfort L (2005) Risk, security, and disaster management. Annu Rev Polit Sci 8:335–356. Available at: https://www.annualreviews.org/doi/pdf/. https://doi.org/10.1146/annurev.polisci.8.081404.075608. Accessed 25 May 2021
6. U.S. Department of Justice (2018) Cyber report—attorney general. Available at: https://www.justice.gov/archives/ag/page/file/1076696/download. Accessed 25 May 2021
7. Sagan S (2004) The problem of redundancy problem: why more nuclear security forces may produce less nuclear security. Available at: http://citeseerx.ist.psu.edu/viewdoc/download?doi=10.1.1.128.3515&rep=rep1&type=pdf. Accessed 25 May 2021

8. Dowell AM, Hendersot DC (2004) No good deed goes unpunished: case studies of incidents and potential incidents caused by protective systems. Proc Safety Prog 16:132–139
9. International Atomic Energy Agency (2020) Incident and trafficking database: incidents of nuclear and other radioactive material out of regulatory control Available at: https://www.iaea.org/sites/default/files/20/02/itdb-factsheet-2020.pdf. Accessed 25 May 2021
10. Siemens and Ponemon Institute (2019) Caught in the crosshairs: are utilities keeping up with cyber threats? Siemens and Ponemon Institute. Available at: https://assets.new.siemens.com/siemens/assets/api/uuid:35089d45-e1c2-4b8b-b4e9-7ce8cae81eaa/version:1572434569/siemens-cybersecurity.pdf. Accessed 25 May 2021
11. Perlroth N (2017) Hackers are targeting nuclear facilities, Homeland Security Dept and F.B.I. Say. The New York Times. Available at: https://www.nytimes.com/2017/07/06/technology/nuclear-plant-hack-report.html. Accessed 25 May 2021
12. Debak D (2019) An Indian nuclear power plant suffered a cyberattack. here's what you need to know. The Washington Post, Available at: https://www.washingtonpost.com/politics/2019/11/04/an-indian-nuclear-power-plant-suffered-cyberattack-heres-what-you-need-know/. Accessed 25 May 2021
13. Check Point Software Technologies Ltd (2020) Increase in remote working and coronavirus related threats creating perfect storm of security challenges for organizations, New Survey Finds. Available at: https://www.checkpoint.com/press/2020/increase-in-remote-working-and-coronavirus-related-threats-creating-perfect-storm-of-security-challenges-for-organizations-new-survey-finds/. Accessed 15 May 2021
14. Sanger D et al (2021) Cyberattack forces a shutdown of a top U.S. pipeline. The New York Times. Available at: https://www.nytimes.com/2021/05/08/us/politics/cyberattack-colonial-pipeline.html. Accessed 25 May 2021
15. International Atomic Energy Agency (2020) Emerging technologies workshop: insights & actionable ideas for key safeguards challenges. Available at: https://www.iaea.org/sites/default/files/20/06/emerging-tehnologies-workshop-290120.pdf. Accessed 25 May 2021
16. United Nations Office of Information and Communications Technology (2018) Blockchain what does it mean for the UN. Available at: https://unite.un.org/sites/unite.un.org/files/emerging-tech-series-blockchain.pdf. Accessed 25 May 2021
17. National Institute of Standards and Technology (2020) Zero trust cybersecurity: never trust, always verify. Available at: https://www.nist.gov/blogs/taking-measure/zero-trust-cybersecurity-never-trust-always-verify. Accessed 25 May 2021.
18. International Atomic Energy Agency (2015) Use of nuclear material accounting and control for nuclear security purposes for facilities. Nuclear Security Series No. 25-G. Available at: https://www-pub.iaea.org/MTCD/Publications/PDF/Pub1685web-43244937.pdf. Accessed 10 May 2021
19. International Atomic Energy Agency (2010) The interface between safety and security at nuclear power plants, INSAG-24. Available at: https://www-pub.iaea.org/MTCD/publications/PDF/Pub1472_web.pdf. Accessed 10 May 2021
20. U.S. Department of Energy Office of Inspector General Office of Audits and Inspections (2012) Special report: inquiry into the security breach at the national nuclear security administration's Y-12 National Security Complex. https://www.energy.gov/sites/prod/files/IG-0868_0.pdf. Accessed 10 May 2021
21. Tsukimori O (2021) Tepco lapse a wake-up call for Japan's nuclear security protocols, expert says, The Japan Times. Available at: https://www.japantimes.co.jp/news/2021/04/15/national/nra-niigata-tepco-nuclear-security/. Accessed 25 May 2021
22. Nobles C (2018) Shifting the human factors paradigm in cybersecurity. Available at: https://csrc.nist.gov/CSRC/media/Events/Federal-Information-Systems-Security-Educators-As/documents/17.pdf; Nuclear Threat Initiative, Addressing the Human Factor: Insider Threats and Security Culture, https://www.ntiindex.org/story/addressing-the-human-factor-insider-threats-and-security-culture/. Accessed 25 May 2021
23. International Atomic Energy Agency (2011) Convention to the physical protection of nuclear material. Available at: https://www.iaea.org/publications/documents/conventions/convention-physical-protection-nuclear-material. Accessed 25 May 2021

24. International Atomic Energy Agency (2011) Nuclear security recommendations on physical protection of nuclear material and nuclear facilities, Nuclear Security Series No. 13. Available at: https://www-pub.iaea.org/MTCD/Publications/PDF/Pub1481_web.pdf. Accessed 25 May 2021

25. Rouhani S, Pourheidari V, Deters R (2019) Physical access control management system based on permissioned blockchain. Available at: https://www.researchgate.net/publication/330700808_Physical_Access_Control_Management_System_Based_on_Permissioned_Blockchain. Accessed 25 May 2021

26. Kaplan D (2020) Why cold chain tracking and IoT sensors are vital to the success of a COVID-19 vaccine. Supply Chain Dive. Available at: https://www.supplychaindive.com/news/coronavirus-vaccine-cold-chain-tracking-iot-sensor-technology/583168/. Accessed 25 May 2021.

27. Zaffran M et al (2012) The imperative for stronger vaccine supply and logistics systems. Vaccine 31S:B73–80

28. Blockcerts: the open standard for blockchain credentials. Available at: https://www.blockcerts.org/about.html. Accessed 25 May 2021

29. Salah K (2017) Internet-of-Things (IoT) security: review, blockchain solutions, and open challenges. Available at: https://www.researchgate.net/publication/321017113_IoT_Security_Review_Blockchain_Solutions_and_Open_Challenges. Accessed 25 May 20

30. World Institute for Nuclear Security (2019) 1.7 corporate governance and legal liability for nuclear facilities. Available at: https://wins.org/document/1-7-corporate-governance-and-legal-liability-for-nuclear-security/. Accessed 25 May 2021

31. Van Dine A et al (2016) Outpacing cyber threats: priorities for cybersecurity at nuclear facilities. Nuclear Threat Initiative. Available at: https://media.nti.org/documents/NTI_CyberThreats__FINAL.pdf. Accessed 25 May 2021

32. Baylon C, Brunt R, Livingstone D (2015) Cyber security at civil nuclear facilities: understanding the risks Chatham House. Available at: https://www.chathamhouse.org/sites/default/files/field/field_document/20151005CyberSecurityNuclearBaylonBruntLivingstone.pdf. Accessed 25 May 2021

33. Conte de Leon D et al (2017) Blockchain properties and misconceptions. Asia Pacific J Innovation Entrepreneurship 11(3):286–300

34. Umayam ML, Vestergaard C (2020) Complementing the padlock: the prospect of blockchain for strengthening nuclear security, Stimson Center, Available at: https://www.stimson.org/2020/complementing-the-padlock-the-prospect-of-blockchain-for-strengthening-nuclear-security/. Accessed on 26 May 2021

35. Taylor P et al (2020) A systematic literature review of blockchain cyber security. Digital Commun Network 6:147–156

36. Halamka J (2017) The potential for blockchain to transform electronic health records. Available at: https://hbr.org/2017/03/the-potential-for-blockchain-to-transform-electronic-health-records. Accessed 26 May 2021

37. International Atomic Energy Agency (2011) Nuclear security recommendations on physical protection of nuclear material and nuclear facilities. Nuclear Security Series No. 13, Available at: https://www-pub.iaea.org/MTCD/Publications/PDF/Pub1481_web.pdf. Accessed 26 May 2021

38. World Nuclear Transport Institute (2021) Nuclear transport facts. https://www.wnti.co.uk/nuclear-transport-facts/facts-figures.aspx; https://www.wnti.co.uk/wp-content/uploads/2021/01/Quick-Facts-on-the-Transport-of-Nuclear-Fuel-Cycle-Transport.pdf. Accessed 26 May 2021

39. Nuclear Energy Institute (2019) Safe, secure transportation of used nuclear fuel. Available at: https://www.nei.org/resources/fact-sheets/safe-secure-transportation-used-nuclear-fuel. Accessed 26 May 2021

40. Williams AD (2016) A new look at transportation security: a complex risk mitigation framework for the security of international spent nuclear fuel transportation. Available at: https://www.osti.gov/servlets/purl/1409912. Accessed 26 May 2021

41. Simpson C (2013) They found the stolen truck filled with radioactive material. The Atlantic, Available at: https://www.theatlantic.com/international/archive/2013/12/radioactive-material-stolen-mexico-worries-iaea/355773/. Accessed 17 May 2021
42. Imeri A, Khadraoui D (2018) The security and traceability of shared information in the process of transportation of dangerous goods. In: Paper presented at the 9th IFIP international conference on new technologies, mobility and security (NTMS). Available at: https://ieeexplore.ieee.org/abstract/document/8328751/metrics#metrics. Accessed 26 May 2021
43. Dobrovnik M et al (2018) Blockchain for and in logistics: what to adopt and where to start. Logistics, MDPI 2(18):1–14
44. DeBeers Group Tracr, Available at: https://www.debeersgroup.com/building-forever/leading-ethical-practices-across-industry/tracr. Accessed 26 May 2021
45. Transport Topics (2018) Blockchain for trucking. Available at: https://www.ttnews.com/articles/blockchain-trucking. Accessed 26 May 2021
46. Guardtime and EY (2018) Press Release: World's first blockchain platform for marine insurance now in commercial use. Available at: https://www.ey.com/en_gl/news/2018/05/world-s-first-blockchain-platform-for-marine-insurance-now-in-co. Accessed 20 September 2021
47. Gaur V, Gaiha A (2020) Building a transparent supply chain: blockchain can enhance trust, efficiency, and speed. Harvard Business Review Available at: https://hbr.org/2020/05/building-a-transparent-supply-chain. Accessed 26 May 2021
48. Tradelens, Accelerate Your Move to a Fully Digital Port. Available at: https://www.tradelens.com/ecosystem/ports-and-terminals. Accessed 26 May 2021
49. CBR Tech Monitor(2019) Computer business review. Available at: https://www.cbronline.com/news/tradelens-data. Accessed 26 May 2021

Blockchain for Global Trade in Dual-Use Chemicals

Richard T. Cupitt

Abstract There is an ever-growing need to strengthen the measures preventing the proliferation of chemical weapons, especially in improving the controls on dual-use chemicals. These dual-use chemicals often have legitimate commercial uses, but may be used by proliferators and terrorists as chemical weapons or precursors to create chemical weapons. This chapter aims to assess how and where DLT may be most effective by analyzing both the Chemical Weapons Convention (CWC) and multilateral efforts. First, there is an analysis of the trade control obligations of the CWC and its related international information flows to assess where DLT may be most useful. Second, the chapter reviews multilateral efforts to control dual-use chemicals by looking specifically at the Australia Group and its related international information flows in order to evaluate where DLT may be most valuable. Additionally, this section will consider how the work of the Australia Group and the CWC might connect. Finally, this chapter aims to highlight how the use of existing DLT platforms may be used as an initial proof of concept for a DLT-based solution for dual-use chemical trade controls by examining the case of end-user certificates.

1 Introduction

In April 2017, about 100 men, women and children in Khan Shaykhun died from a sarin gas attack perpetrated by the Syrian government [1]. Unfortunately, this was not an isolated event. In the 1980s, the extensive use of chemical weapons in the Iran-Iraq war prompted many major chemical supplier countries to band together (such as in the Australia Group, a multilateral export control regime) to prevent the export of key chemical weapons precursors to suspect end-users. Who are suspect end-users? The Australia Group currently indicates that controls will "affect only sales to a small number of countries" where evidence suggests interest in having a chemical or biological weapons "capacity" or constitute a risk of diversion to terroritsts [2].

R. T. Cupitt (✉)
The Henry L. Stimson Center, Washington, DC, USA
e-mail: rcupitt@stimson.org

© Springer Nature Switzerland AG 2021

C. Vestergaard (ed.), *Blockchain for International Security*,
Advanced Sciences and Technologies for Security Applications,
https://doi.org/10.1007/978-3-030-86240-4_6

With the end of the Cold War, the international community went on to ban the use, production, etc., of chemicals (including sarin) as weapons through the 1993 Chemical Weapons Convention (CWC), which came into force in 1997. Since then, the international community has seen the dismantlement of state chemical weapons programs and their stockpiles, under the watchful monitoring of the Organisation for the Prohibition of Chemical Weapons (OPCW). With the exception of the Aum Shinrikyo sarin gas attack on the Tokyo Subway system in 1995, the use of chemicals as weapons by non-state actors generally remained small-scale if persistent. However, this small-scale use changed significantly when both the Syrian government and ISIS began using chemical weapons. Since then, the number of countries worldwide experiencing chemical terrorism has increased sharply [3, 4].

A question remains, though, of how states or non-state actors aquire chemical weapons if the CWC bans their production and trade. At its simplest, these actors either use dual-use chemicals as weapons or as precursors to weapons. Dual-use items include goods, technologies, or services that have mainly commercial, but also military applications. There are a plethora of chemicals that fall into this category. For example, in February 2019 the Penal Court of Antwerp fined three Flemish companies and imposed prison sentences on two of their managers for exporting 168 tons of highly pure isopropanol to Syria, which the European Union had explicitly forbidden [5]. Therein lies another question—How did Flemish companies illicitly export highly pure isopropanol to Syria without raising red flags across the European Union? Part of the answer is that isopropanol has many other common, peaceful uses, such as being used as a solvent, an astringent, a cleaning agent, and more. The average person has likely used isopropanol in a peaceful manner. When combined with water, isopropanol becomes rubbing alcohol. However, in a highly pure concentration, combining isopropanol with methylphosphonyl difluoride is the final step in the main process for producing sarin, a chemical weapon [6]. Covering around 20 separate shipments, this court case exposed significant shortcomings in Belgian customs and export control authorities in implementing controls, as the exports only came to light through the work of investigative journalists looking at trade statistics [5].

A wide body of literature exists on how companies and other stakeholders can use distributed ledger technology (DLT) in international trade and supply chain management, also discussed elsewhere in this book [7–9]. Moreover, several studies argue that DLT has considerable promise in the realm of nonproliferation export controls [10–12]. This chapter focuses on DLT's considerable promise for (1) improving the management of trade in dual-use chemicals of interest specifically; (2) if implemented, dissuading illicit shipments or, at least, creating an immediate awareness of such transactions to authorities; and (3) helping to trace the provenance of the materials for identifying and prosecuting culpable parties. Thus, this chapter aims to assess how and where DLT may be most effective by analyzing both the CWC and multilateral efforts. First, there is an analysis of the trade control obligations of the CWC and its related international information flows to assess where DLT may be most useful. Second, the chapter reviews multilateral efforts to control dual-use chemicals by looking specifically at the Australia Group and its related international information flows in order to evaluate where DLT may be most valuable. Additionally, this section will consider how the work of the Australia Group and the CWC might need to connect. Finally, this chapter aims to highlight how the use of existing DLT platforms may be used as an initial proof of concept for a DLT-based solution for dual-use chemical trade controls by examining the case of end-user certificates.

2 The CWC and Its Schedules: Obligations and Information Flows

Although the CWC applies to any toxic chemical used as a weapon, in practice the CWC aims to control a subset of toxic chemicals, as first noted in Article VI ("Activities Not Prohibited Under This Convention"):

> To this end, and in order to verify that activities are in accordance with obligations under this Convention, each State Party shall subject toxic chemicals and their precursors listed in Schedules 1, 2 and 3 of the Annex on Chemicals ... to verification measures as provided in the Verification Annex [13].

State Parties must also provide a list of facilities that produce more than 200 tons of *unscheduled* discrete organic chemicals (i.e., compounds of carbon except for oxides, sulfides, and metal carbonates) or more than 30 tons of such chemicals containing fluorine, phosphorus, or sulfur [14]. The CWC does not, however, require restrictions or reporting on transfers of these chemicals.

The Schedules are based on at least two underlying factors: chemicals that have been used in chemical weapons programs in the past and the extent of the chemical's legitimate commercial uses. The scale of the chemical industry and its integration into modern life makes the second factor particularly important and makes the management issues in preventing the proliferation of chemical weapons more challenging than trade in rarer commodities, such as special nuclear materials. The value of the global chemical industry, for example, was estimated to be USD $5 trillion in 2017, making it the fifth-largest manufacturing sector. Chemicals have a smaller but still significant share of the global world merchandise trade, which the WTO estimated at USD $19.67 trillion in 2018, at about USD $581.8 billion [15, 16].

Schedule 1A toxic chemicals, such as sarin, along with four Schedule 1B precursor chemicals, all essentially have no or extremely limited commercial or other legitimate uses. The CWC allows transfers of these chemicals to other State Parties only for research, medical, pharmaceutical or protective purposes, and no transfers to third States [16]. However, the State Party should declare any transfers for the prior calendar year, including information on the receiving or sending States [17].

In contrast, Schedule 2A*, 2A and 2B chemicals have some legitimate uses. The CWC requires State Parties declare in aggregate imports and exports of Schedule 2 chemicals over certain thresholds of weight and concentrations by the calendar year to the OPCW [18].[1] However, the Convention included an incentive in that 3 years after its entry into force, transfers of such chemicals could only take place between State Parties, an incentive for universalization of the convention.

Finally, Schedule 3 chemicals have widespread commercial uses. State Parties must declare in aggregate to the OPCW the import and export of 30 tons or more at or above a concentration threshold of 30% by the calendar year [18]. The declarations should specify "the sending or the receiving State" of such chemicals [18]. State Parties can authorize transfers to States not Party, as long as the recipient State provides a certificate assuring appropriate use and no re-transfer of the chemicals, along with information on the chemical type and amount and on their end-use and end-user (e.g., an End-User Certificate (EUC) [19]. As the CWC has become nearly universal, this process has become much less relevant.

The CWC created the Organisation for the Prohibition of Chemical Weapons (OPCW) as its main body for implementing the verification measures, e.g., the declarations. The primary information flows go between domestic entities and the national authorities, which is where DLT might prove most useful. At the international level, however, the main information flows are annual declarations to the OPCW regarding scheduled chemicals. In addition to getting State Parties to adopt appropriate domestic legal instruments to implement their CWC obligations and make timely declarations, the OPCW faces a particularly difficult task in reconciling national declarations on exports and imports between sending and recipient countries, known as "transfer discrepancies" [20].

In recent years, about 70% of the declared transfers of chemicals above the thresholds suffer from discrepancies between the data declared by the sending and receiving States, of which the OPCW can resolve only about a tenth [21]. This is one challenge facing the OPCW in which DLT may offer a solution. If only a few countries engaged in the export and import of CWC Scheduled chemicals, these transfer discrepancies might be an easier problem to solve. In reality, there are dozens of State Parties trading in CWC Scheduled chemicals, all subject to reporting. For example, the most traded chemical on the OCPW's "List of Most Traded Chemicals," Mixture of (5-ethyl-2-methyl-2-oxido-1,3,2-dioxaphosphinan-5-yl) methyl methyl methylphosphonate (CAS RN 41203-81-0) and Bis[(5-Ethyl-2-methyl-2-oxido-1,3,2-dioxaphosphinan-5-yl)methyl] methylphosphonate (CAS RN 42595-45-9, with HS Code correlation as 382491) was traded by at least 109 UN Member States, including 78 states reporting exports, based on UN COMTRADE data for the years 2015–2019 [21, 22]. Even the sixth most traded chemical, Dimethyl methylphosphonate (CAS RN 756-79-6, with HS Code correlation as 293131) was traded by at least 44 UN Member States, with 15 listed as exporters [22, 23]. And among State Parties, 4,855 industrial facilities are subject to inspection by the OPCW, which is likely a low estimate given the challenges countries face in determining the number of such facilities in their jurisdiction [18, 24].

---

[1] Specifically, declarations cover imports and exports of 1 kg of a Schedule 2A* chemical, 100 kg of a Schedule 2A chemical, and 1 ton of a Schedule 2B chemical, at concentrations of 1% of a 2A*, 1% of a 2A, and 30% of a 2B chemical.

If one could make reliable links with general international trade data, one might also solve the problem of transfer discrepancies. Unfortunately, there are huge asymmetries in most trade statistics stemming from different methods of calculating, recording and reporting trade data across and between national jurisdictions [25–27]. At times, such asymmetries have even led some to conclude malfeasance where none existed [28]. In the context of the CWC, the discrepancies might reveal ineffective national controls or lack of harmonized reporting. More importantly, the inability to resolve transfer discrepancies could mask efforts by a State Party (or even a non-state actor within a State) to foster a chemical weapons program or lead some State Parties to believe, falsely, that other State Parties harbour such ambitions.

As with the larger trade data asymmetries problem, it is likely that CWC transfer discrepancies arise from several sources. For example, the European Union and other economic communities where goods, technology and services move freely within the community make tracking the origin and destination of imports and exports inherently challenging. More broadly, transfers from one State into a free trade zone in another State might not be seen as a transfer by the latter. Subsequently, such a transfer might not even be acknowledged as having taken place and might be moved on to other States. Similarly, a State may have multiple imports of a controlled chemical below the transfer threshold that in aggregate put it in a position to declare, whereas the associate exporting States might not need to report as the level of their individual transactions would not meet the reporting threshold. The annual character of the data also means that an export in one year might not arrive in the recipient State Party until the next year.

Making this more difficult, many chemicals of concern have multiple names (in some cases, hundreds) or multiple tariff codes (although the CWC's most traded chemicals are each linked with one HS code, the codes only go to six digits, so several of them have the same HS code or industry uses multiple HS codes at eight or ten digit levels used by many customs administrations). Although each of the most traded CWC chemical has a single Chemical Abstracts Service (CAS) Registry Number, Costanzi et al., point out, "the fact that a registry number is not included in a list does not guarantee that the chemical identified by the number is not just a different form of a controlled chemical" [29].

In consideration of the challenges surrounding transfer discrepanices of Scheduled chemicals, a question arises of whether DLT may offer a solution. Certainly, the overall information flows involve multiple and differing types of parties from exporters, importers, national authorities, and for the international flows, the OPCW (see Fig. 1). Currently, each plant provides its longitude and latitude along with other helpful location information, the chemical product groups it uses, and the amounts and country source or destination of imports and exports respectively. Information goes from the plant to the national authority to the OPCW, who will engage national authorities to resolve any discrepancies in a national declaration and between national declarations. This argues for a secure information system that would allow access by multiple stakeholders in near real time.

In 2012, the OPCW began developing its Secure Information Exchange (SIX) system to create a more efficient, timely and secure end-to-end encrypted electronic

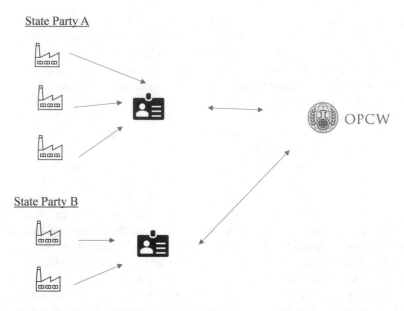

State Party A

State Party B

Fig. 1 Hypothetical flows of CWC declaration information on scheduled chemicals

means of submitting declarations, meant to replace the system of submitting declarations physically by diplomatic pouch [30]. More recently, the OPCW has developed its Electronic Declaration Information System (EDIS), which replaced the Electronic Declaration tool for National Authorities (EDNA) introduced in 2007. EDIS is a distributed multi-access system to help national authorities in preparing, finalizing, analyzing, and working with the OPCW in verifying their declarations, all of which should make reporting more accurate, timely, and secure [31].

What these tools do not do, however, is resolve transfer discrepancies between national declarations. In addition to the issues of timeliness and security, the confidentiality of the data is increasingly important, particularly where a State Party has only a small number of chemical importers and exporters, such that trade data can reveal significant proprietary market and other information if made available to competitors. The OPCW is working to create more tools that in a permissioned DLT system would allow access to data by a range of internal and external actors, including the private sector. A permissioned DLT system would also mean that everyone would work from the same data ("ledger"), flag any ledger changes while making previously entered data immutable, create opportunities to standardize and automate reporting, and more. A permissioned DLT system could also integrate with SIX, EDIS, and new domestic tools that, for example, might allow for near real-time entries that could help the OPCW identify and resolve automatically some of the discrepancies caused by the calendar year reporting requirements or data aggregation issues while not impairing the confidentiality of national submissions.

In addition to the OPCW, national authorities who are licensing the import or export of Scheduled chemicals may have systems in place that would benefit from an enhanced chain-of-custody DLT system. This may be especially beneficial where individual importers or exporters have their own chain-of-custody systems. For example, exporters could enter their licensing and declaration-related information for the shipment of a scheduled chemical into a blockchain, where each jurisdiction that sees the shipment could register it through to its final receipt. Thus, this could strengthen the collective effectiveness of the export control systems of the individual jurisdictions. Moreover, the OPCW could have permissioned access to the record of exports and receipt, perhaps with automatic reconciliation matching sending and receiving data that the national authorities could use to submit declarations, that could further verification and trust in the CWC.

The national authorities for the CWC, however, are often not the national authorities that do the day-to-day licensing of chemical imports and exports. Rather than using the OPCW, the Australia Group serves as the institutional nexus for most of the licensing authorites among key chemical supplier countries. Although some members of the CWC question the existence of the Australia Group, its use of DLT licensing and reporting systems, if done in ways that complement any OPCW systems, would help resolve some of the causes of transfer discrepencies and help achieve the objectives of the CWC in preventing chemical weapons proliferation.

3   The Australia Group and Its Lists: Guidance

Many States have at least some level of controls on trade in the Scheduled chemicals. In the Final Document from the 2016 Comprehensive Review of UN Security Council resolution 1540 (2004), for example, the 1540 Committee found that 112 UN Member States have licensing provisions and 108 have control lists related to chemicals of proliferation concern [32]. A quick perusal of the 1540 Committee country matrices indicates that most of these control lists cover the CWC Schedules. However, the most extensively developed national export control systems for chemicals of proliferation concern exist among the participants of the Australia Group, an informal multilateral organization established in 1985, well before the CWC [33, 34].[2] The extensive use of chemical weapons in the Iran-Iraq war, where Iraq accessed some materials through trade in dual-use items, prompted a number of supplier countries to create common lists of items that should be subject to national export controls, develop common guidance on how to exercise controls, and engage in information exchanges on a range of topics, such as risks and licensing practices. These activities were similar to other multilateral supplier groups, e.g., the Nuclear Suppliers Group and the Missile Technology Control Regime. The Australia Group maintains five lists of controlled

---

[2] As of January 2021, the Australia Group has 43 participants: Argentina; Australia; Austria; Belgium; Bulgaria; Canada; Croatia; Czechia; Denmark; Estonia; European Union; Finland; France; Germany; Greece; Hungary; Iceland; India; Ireland; Italy; Japan; Latvia; Lithuania; Luxembourg; Malta; Mexico; Netherlands; New Zealand; Norway; Poland; Portugal; Republic of Cyprus; Republic of Korea; Republic of Turkey; Romania; Slovak Republic; Slovenia; Spain; Sweden; Switzerland; Ukraine; United Kingdom; and the United States.

items. The most relevant of which for this chapter is the list of Chemical Weapons Precursors [35].

The Australia Group Guidelines called on participants to deny transfers if they judged that the (listed) items would go to a chemical or biological weapons program, be used for chemical or biological weapons terrorism, or pose a significant risk of diversion to such ends. Here one can see another opportunity for using a permissioned DLT system, which could make sharing of data on denials more timely, immutable, and secure, with everyone having access to the same data. The Guidelines also had participants exercise controls on re-exports and require authorizations for non-listed items under certain conditions (e.g., catch-all controls). Participants have considerable discretion in implementing the controls, including remaining fully free to apply additional national-level controls. However, they must also abide by a "no undercut" rule, such that if one participant denied a license of a listed item, another participant would not approve the transfer of an "essentially identical" license without prior consultations with the denying government or after the expiration or rescinding of the denial. In addition to its 42 participants (plus the European Union) and one "adherent" (Kazakhstan), several other countries use the Australia Group lists, which are openly available to all, in their control systems (e.g., Malaysia, Singapore). Many other countries also use the European Union (EU) control lists as a basis for their own control lists and by doing so indirectly adhere to the Australia Group lists.

Most of the information flows for Australia Group participants take place at the national level, between the licensing authority (which may or may not be the same as the enforcement authority, e.g., customs, border guards, or police) and the exporter in the process of granting the license or implementing the conditions of the license. Participants do share amongst themselves information on license denials, on re-export assurances, and, in practice, enforcement matters. Outside of license denials, cross-boundary licensing information flows are not through the Australia Group, but with documents supporting the shipment as it passes through multiple jurisdictions. In particular, export controls depend on verifying end-users and licensing documents, which in many jurisdictions remain paper bound, and have been exploited notoriously through falsifying key documents. These are practices that DLT might help curtail. Cándano (2020) argues, for example, that the use of smart contracts could prevent payment for a shipment if an unauthorized alteration of a licence took place [36]. None of these potential benefits from DLT will occur automatically. It will require intelligent data design to meet a range of requirements, such as adhering to applicable right to be forgotten laws, and contract designs that take into account that transforming current processes into fully integrated supply chain management systems will likely need a phased, long-term approach.

4 DLT and Export Controls: A Practical Example for Chemical End-User Assurances for Re-exports

End-user certificates are one area in particular that DLT may prove effective. As noted above, the Australia Group Guidelines calls on its participants to exercise control over re-export, including where needed to "obtain satisfactory assurances that its consent will be secured prior to any retransfer to a third country," usually in the form of an official document, e.g., an end-user certificate (EUC) [37]. Similarly, the CWC requires State Parties to obtain a certificate of assurance from non-State Parties for the transfer of Schedule 3 chemicals (although this has become far less important with universalization of the treaty). For decades, governments have used some variation of EUCs as an important assurance tool. Typically, an EUC contains such assurances from the end-user or governing authority of the jurisdiction where the end-user resides. Legitimate exporters and intermediaries may also want similar assurances to protect their reputations, avoid legal liabilities, as well as to prevent proliferation. Proliferators or less legitimate exporters, intermediaries, or end-users attempt to subvert these assurances through fake or falsified EUCs [36]. As DLT mechanisms are particularly useful in securing the digital identity of a document, DLT could curb use of fake or falsified EUCs for dual-use chemical precursors.

In the instance of fake or falsified EUCs, a solution needs to increase trust in the integrity of these documents that involve multiple parties from different cultures and jurisdictions for thousands of transactions. Many current DLT projects address this very problem, validating credentials and provenance for a wide audience for large numbers of transactions (for some examples, see [38–40]). This suggests that DLT could prove useful for the EUC process. Enhancing trust across stakeholders stands as perhaps the most important contribution of any DLT system. For EUCs, a simple DLT system could enhance trust during three phases: engaging the end-user; verifying the documents; and verifying the issuer.

The process would begin by the exporter (or the governing authority for the exporter's jurisdiction) requesting an EUC for an export license application for, let us say a chemical from the CWC Schedules, from the governing authority of the importer, where upon the governing authority (or less often, the end-user) issues an EUC assuring the chemicals appropriate end-use. Using a DLT system, the issuing body could create an EUC as a digital asset with a digital fingerprint (hash) for the asset, uploading the latter to the ledger. To verify the EUC, the issuer sends the digital EUC asset to the requesting government entity or exporter. The requester uses the digital signature to probe the distributed ledger. This provides assurance that the EUC exists.

In the last steps of the process, the requesting government examines the URL in the digital signature for the EV SSL Certificate associated with the URL. The requester would then evaluate the EV SSL Certificate to decide whether to trust or not trust that the document came from an approved or recognized issuing governing authority or end-user, a process one might automate. Finally, the requester includes the EUC as a supporting document for the authority evaluating export license applications and issuing license approvals.

With DLT, the licensing authority and exporter can check the validity of the EUC and also check the EUC against other criteria, such as the time from issuance. The added advantage of immutability not only makes the record more secure itself, but any changes to the document provide a solid audit trail and, if needed, an important tool for forensic accounting in any investigation or prosecution. This proposed solution has the advantage of integrating DLT into an existing bureaucratic process requiring relatively minor adaptations, if any, by stakeholders to gain significant added value, while using existing technologies. No system, of course, prevents government authorities from issuing assurances that they will not or cannot keep, but a distributed ledger system for EUCs could make it harder for illicit exploitation of EUCs.

5 Conclusion

While DLT lends itself as a promising technology for the OPCW and the Australia Group, there are still barriers to its implementation and challenges to be considered. For instance, if the Australia Group were to pursue a DLT system for the OPCW that depended on the national export control systems of the Australia Group participants, this would require considerable sensitivity. One reason for this is that several State Parties to the CWC, once in force, have argued that the Australia Group is discriminatory and have called for its abandonment. Yet, challenges like this should not deter the technology itself from being considered. With more than 40 key supplier participants, all State Parties to the CWC, building on this network of national authorities through DLT offers a promising way forward to resolving (1) transfer discrepancies and (2) a host of issues related to verification of documents related to transfers of dual-use chemicals.

With the Syrian chemical attacks at the forefront of recent events, it is clear that there has been a resurgence of chemical weapons use by States and non-state actors alike. Thus, the time for considering DLT is more relevant than ever as DLT has the potential to strengthen international efforts preventing the proliferation of chemical weapons and protecting the legitimate commercial and scientific transfers of dual-use chemicals of proliferation concern. The international community can employ strengths of DLT systems, especially transparency and accountability, to counter the obfuscation, misdirection, and mistrust that proliferators use to deflect culpability.

References

1. Organisation for the Prohibition of Chemical Weapons (OPCW)-United Nations Joint Investigative Mechanism (2017) Seventh report of the Organisation for the Prohibition of Chemical Weapons-United Nations Joint Investigative Mechanism, S/2017/904. https://www.securityc ouncilreport.org/atf/cf/%7B65BFCF9B-6D27-4E9C-8CD3-CF6E4FF96FF9%7D/s_2017_904.pdf. Accessed 27 May 2021
2. Australia Group (2021) The Australia Group and legitimate trade. Australian Department of Foreign Affairs and Trade. https://www.dfat.gov.au/publications/minisite/theaustraliagro upnet/site/en/trade.html. Accessed 27 May 2021
3. Binder MK, Ackerman GA (2019) Pick your POICN: introducing the profiles of incidents involving CBRN and non-state actors (POICN) Database. Studies in Conflict & Terrorism. https://www.tandfonline.com/doi/full/10.1080/1057610X.2019.1577541. Accessed 27 May 2021
4. Cupitt RT (2017) Developing indices to measure chemical strategic trade security controls. Strat Trade Rev 41–70
5. Marks S (2019) Belgian exporters found guilty of sending chemicals to Syria: two executives receive jail terms. Politico. https://www.politico.eu/article/belgian-exporters-found-guilty-of-sending-chemicals-to-syria/. Accessed 27 May 2021
6. Abou-Donia MB et al (2016) Sarin (GB, O-isopropyl methylphosphonofluoridate) neurotoxicity: critical review. Crit Rev Toxicol 46(10):845–875. https://doi.org/10.1080/10408444.2016.1220916 Accessed 27 May 2021
7. Ganne E (2018) Can blockchain revolutionize world trade? World Trade Organization, Geneva. https://www.wto.org/english/res_e/publications_e/blockchainrev18_e.htm. Accessed 10 June 2021
8. Fefer RF (2019) Blockchain and international trade. In: Focus. IF10810, Version 4, Updated. Congressional Research Service, Washington, DC
9. Kerstens J, Canham J (2018) Blockchain: mapping new trade routes to trust. https://mag.wco omd.org/magazine/wco-news-87/blockchain-mapping-new-trade-routes-to-trust/. Accessed 27 May 2021
10. Coscarella C, Minotti A (2020) An institutional blockchain as a tool to control the export of dual-use and military goods. Strat Trade Rev 6:93–112
11. Ryan S, Majid F (2018) Blockchain and export controls: bridging technology and controls. Deloitte Global Trade Advisory presentation at the WordECR Export Controls and Sanctions Forum. Washington, DC, June 2018
12. Arnold A (2017) Blockchain: a new aid to nuclear export controls? The Bulletin of Atomic Scientists. https://thebulletin.org/blockchain-new-aid-nuclear-export-controls11204. Accessed 27 May 2021
13. Chemical Weapons Convention (2021) Article VI. https://www.opcw.org/chemical-weapons-convention/articles/article-vi-activities-not-prohibited-under-convention. Accessed 27 May 2021
14. OPCW (2021) Declaration requirements for scheduled chemicals. https://www.opcw.org/res ources/declarations/declaration-requirements-scheduled-chemicals. Accessed 27 May 2021
15. World Trade Organization (2019) World Trade statistical review WTO, Geneva, p 8. https:// www.wto.org/english/res_e/statis_e/wts2019_e/wts2019_e.pdf. Accessed 27 May 2021
16. Workman D (2020) Chemical exports by country. www.WorldsTopExports.com (WTEx). http://www.worldstopexports.com/chemical-exports-by-country/. Accessed 27 May 2021
17. CWC (2021) Annex on Implementation and Verification, "Verification Annex," PART VI: activities not prohibited under this Convention in accordance with Article Vi, regime for schedule 1 chemicals and facilities related to such chemicals, B.3. https://www.opcw.org/chemical-wea pons-convention/articles/article-vi-activities-not-prohibited-under-convention. Accessed 27 May 2021

18. OPCW (2013) Declarations handbook (Revised 2017). https://www.opcw.org/sites/default/files/documents/2018/11/Sections%20A%2CB%2CC%2CK%2CL%20and%20M%20%26%20App%201and3%20to%208_0_0.pdf. Accessed 27 May 2021
19. CWC (2021) Annex on Implementation and Verification, "Verification Annex," Part VIII: activities not prohibited under this Convention in accordance with Article Vi, regime for schedule 3 chemicals and facilities related to such chemicals, C.26. https://www.opcw.org/chemical-weapons-convention/annexes/verification-annex/part-viii-regime-schedule-3-chemicals-and. Accessed 27 May 2021
20. Kelle A (2012) Non-proliferation and preventing the re-emergence of chemical weapons. Disarmament Forum 1, pp 55–64, p 61. https://unidir.org/files/publications/pdfs/agent-of-change-the-cw-regime-en-312.pdf. Accessed 27 May 2021
21. Communication with OPCW staff, 20 Feb 2020
22. OPCW (2017) Most traded scheduled chemicals. https://www.opcw.org/resources/declarations/most-traded-scheduled-chemicals-2017. Accessed 27 May 2021
23. United Nations UN COMTRADE database (2021) https://comtrade.un.org/. Accessed 27 May 2021
24. OPCW (2021) OPCW by the numbers (2021) https://www.opcw.org/media-centre/opcw-numbers. Accessed 27 May 2021
25. United Nations Economic and Social Council, Statistical Commission (2015) Report of the friends of the chair group on the measurement of international trade and economic globalization. E/CN.3/2015/12, 14-67368
26. Markhonko V (2014) Asymmetries in official international trade statistics and analysis of globalization. In: Paper presented at the United Nations friends of the chair meeting on the measurement of international trade and economic globalization. Aguascalientes, Mexico, 2 Oct 2014. https://unstats.un.org/unsd/trade/events/2014/mexico/Asymmetries%20in%20official%20ITS%20and%20analysis%20of%20globalization%20-%20V%20Markhonko%20-%202018%20Sep%202014.pdf. Accessed 27 May 2021
27. U.S. Department of Commerce, Office of the United States Trade Representative, and P.R.C. Ministry of Commerce (2009) Report on the statistical discrepancy of merchandise trade between the United States and China. Hangzhou, P.R.C. https://www.commerce.gov/sites/default/files/migrated/reports/statisticaldiscrepancy.pdf. Accessed 27 May 2021
28. Forstater M (2018) Illicit financial flows, trade misinvoicing, and multinational tax avoidance: the same or different? CGD Policy Paper 123. https://www.cgdev.org/publication/illicit-financial-flows-trade-misinvoicing-and-multinational-tax-avoidance. Accessed 27 May 2021
29. Costanzi S, Koblenz GD, Cupitt RT (2020) Leveraging cheminformatics to bolster the control of chemical warfare agents and their precursors. Strat Trade Rev 6:69–92
30. OPCW (2014) "Secure information exchange (SIX)," Note by the Technical Secretariat, S/1192/2014. https://www.opcw.org/sites/default/files/documents/S_series/2014/en/s-1192-2014_e_.pdf. Accessed 27 May 2021
31. OPCW (2021) Electronic Data Information System (EDIS). https://www.opcw.org/resources/declarations/electronic-declaration-information-system-edis. Accessed 27 May 2021
32. Committee established pursuant to United Nations to resolution 1540 (2004) "Report (Final document on the 2016 comprehensive review of the status of implementation of resolution 1540 (2004))," 9 December 2016
33. Australia Group (2021) "The Origins of the Australia Group," Australian Department of Foreign Affairs. https://www.dfat.gov.au/publications/minisite/theaustraliagroupnet/site/en/origins.html. Accessed 27 May 2021
34. Australia Group (2021) "Australia Group Participants," Australian Department of Foreign Affairs. https://www.dfat.gov.au/publications/minisite/theaustraliagroupnet/site/en/participants.html. Accessed 27 May 2021
35. Australia Group (2021) Export control list: chemical weapons precursors. https://australiagroup.net/en/precursors.html. Accessed 27 May 2021
36. Cándano D (2020) "Blockchain for export controls," in a commentary for the Blockchain in Practice Program. https://www.stimson.org/2020/blockchain-for-export-controls/. Accessed 27 May 2021

37. Australia Group (2015) "Guidelines for transfers of sensitive chemical or biological items," Article 5. https://australiagroup.net/en/guidelines.html. Accessed 27 May 2021
38. Okazaki Y (2018) "Unveiling the potential of blockchain for customs," WCO Research Paper No. 45, June 2018. http://www.wcoomd.org/-/media/wco/public/global/pdf/topics/research/research-paper-series/45_yotaro_okazaki_unveiling_the_potential_of_blockchain_for_customs.pdf?la=en. Accessed 27 May 2021
39. del Castillo M (2019) "Blockchain goes to work at Walmart, IBM, Amazon, JPMorgan, Cargill and 46 other enterprises," Forbes. https://www.forbes.com/sites/michaeldelcastillo/2019/04/16/blockchain-goes-to-work/. Accessed 27 May 2021
40. Morris N (2018) Singapore-backed global trade blockchain launches. Ledger Insights. https://www.ledgerinsights.com/singapore-trade-blockchain-otb/. Accessed 27 May 2021

Blockchain Applications for Export Control Compliance and Global Supply Chain Integrity

Diego Cándano Laris

Abstract Export controls are an essential tool of the international security architecture and play an important role in protecting the supply chain of sensitive items. Governments and industry face important challenges implementing export controls, but there are also incentives for exporters compliance, which include avoiding reputational damage and protecting intellectual property. Blockchain is already being used to protect the supply chain integrity in specific industries. Three potential applications in the field of export controls are: sensitive data management; detection and prevention of falsified documents and validation of identities; and traceability of sensitive items. This technology can support effective implementation of export controls and help government and industry benefit in this process.

1 Introduction

Effective export controls contribute to international security by ensuring that strategic military and dual-use goods and technologies are not diverted to unauthorized end-users after crossing borders. Their importance is still most clearly illustrated by the discovery of the A.Q. Khan proliferation network in 2004, which had created a global nuclear black market over decades based on a network that started with some Western companies "willing to exploit lax export controls" and whose fingerprints are still "all over the world's most volatile nuclear hot spots" [1]. The A.Q. Khan case is an emblematic example of how deliberate efforts to circumvent export control laws provided nuclear knowledge and technology to unauthorized users with enormous consequences for global security [2]. Furthermore, it shows that export controls, often considered an obscure and technical component of bureaucratic procedures, play a defining role in securing the supply chains of the most sensitive goods and technologies. This relevance is set to grow as an increasing number of States are

D. Cándano Laris (✉)
The Henry L. Stimson Center, Washington, DC, USA
e-mail: diego@candano.org

© Springer Nature Switzerland AG 2021

C. Vestergaard (ed.), *Blockchain for International Security*,
Advanced Sciences and Technologies for Security Applications,
https://doi.org/10.1007/978-3-030-86240-4_7

89

implementing export controls after they became an international obligation under the United Nations Security Council (UNSC) resolution 1540.

Developing a comprehensive legal system for export controls is not the only major challenge that States face. Once in place, the effective implementation of this system is a considerable undertaking itself. Based on its capacity to increase transparency and efficiency, distributed ledger technology (DLT) offers considerable potential to enable this implementation, particularly as proliferation networks use cyber tools to take advantage of loopholes in export control systems.

This chapter shows that export controls contribute to ensuring the integrity of strategic supply chains by diminishing the risk of diversion of critical goods and technologies, and therefore close an important loophole in the international security architecture. It argues that DLT, of which blockchain is a subset, could improve the effective implementation and enforcement of export controls. Blockchain and DLT applications are already being analyzed as tools to improve the efficiency of trade procedures, and their potential to reduce hurdles associated with paper-heavy regulations has been the subject of recent studies [3–5]. Indeed, as has been shown by previous chapters in this book, some studies have begun to look into potential applications of blockchain for customs procedures and also for export controls [6, 7].[1]

Section 2 of this chapter discusses the basic elements of an export control system and provides relevant background regarding the importance of export controls as a tool to prevent proliferation. It argues that export controls serve non-proliferation purposes and thus help ensure the integrity of the supply chain of sensitive items. Export controls can also play a role in protecting intellectual property (IP) rights, a core interest for industry, and failure to comply with them may have reputational consequences for companies.

Section 3 identifies some of the main challenges for the effective implementation of export controls, both from the perspective of governments and industry.

Section 4 discusses the advantages of DLT and its relevance for export controls. It identifies and discusses three potential applications of DLT to strengthen the effective implementation of export controls: (1) sensitive data management and licensing processes; (2) valid identities and detection and prevention of falsified documents; and (3) traceability of sensitive items. It will be argued that both industry and governments could take steps to adopt DLT-based solutions to improve data management, preserve the integrity of documents and identities, and maintain oversight of the location of relevant items.

---

[1] It is worth highlighting that this chapter addresses some ways in which DLT can support effective implementation of export controls. It does not deal with the ways in which export controls have been applied to securing and controlling digital technologies, encryption or intrusive software.

2 Relevance of Export Controls for International Security

Export controls are based on a mix of laws, regulations, and policies which States implement in order to have the capacity to control the free movement of certain strategic goods and technologies out of their territories.[2] These strategic goods, technologies, and software can be military or "dual-use" items, e.g., they can be used either for civilian or military purposes, including for the development of weapons of mass destruction (WMD) or their means of delivery, such as machine tools, lasers, computers or navigation systems. Export controls are anchored in national regulations and each State determines the specific criteria that govern such controls and identifies conditions for the authorization of a strategic export. In general, controls seek to avoid diversion of exports to unauthorized uses and/or users, including restricting their access to non-state actors and governments of concern, and are used to implement embargoes adopted by the United Nations Security Council (UNSC). In implementing these controls, States seek that strategic exports do not contradict their national security objectives [9, 10].

The regulations that enable export controls often restrict activities such as transit, trans-shipment, and brokering activities [11] and may include provisions on re-exports as well as transfers of controlled technologies to foreign persons without actually crossing borders, so-called "deemed exports" [12]. Exporters can include governments, state-owned companies, private companies, universities, or private researchers and are the front line in implementing the system. By ensuring that exports of sensitive goods and technologies reach authorized end-users and end-uses, export controls contribute to the integrity of strategic supply chains and reduce the risk that these goods can be used for hostile purposes. Export controls are thus at an intersection of trade and security policies and "have led to a new branch of international law which establishes a bridge between international trade law and the law of international security" [13].

Export control systems vary considerably in their design and mode of operation. There is no single approach to setting up an export control system and different countries have designed highly effective systems following significantly different approaches. Nevertheless, an effective export control system usually has a few common elements [8, 14, 15]. For the purposes of this chapter, it is important to highlight that these elements rely on secure management and transfer of information and on auditability of processes, making them suitable for DLT:

Regulatory framework for controls. A legal or regulatory basis enables a government authority to investigate and/or stop transfers of concern. This usually takes

---

[2] While this article refers to the generic "export controls," it could be useful to recall that Dill and Stewart differentiate between *strategic export controls*, which involve laws and related enforcement action to control the movement of goods with a strategic importance out of the territory, *strategic trade controls*, which also include border, transit and trans-shipment controls (and potentially import controls and extraterritorial measures), and a *strategic trade control system,* which aims to help manage the transfer of sensitive materials, technology or equipment that might be used in weapons systems [8].

the form of a basic law and subsequent regulatory tools which enable implementation of the system. Such frameworks identify the relevant government agencies involved in different stages of the process and specify their responsibilities and mechanisms of interagency coordination. Regulatory frameworks define the extent to which the system includes transit, trans-shipment, re-exports and "catch-all" controls (e.g. controls related to items which are not listed if there is suspicion about their potential end-use), as well as provisions that protect the confidentiality of commercial information, while permitting information-sharing with other governments to enhance international efforts against proliferation.

Control lists. The export control regulations must be complemented by lists of goods and technologies which are subject to controls under such regulations. Control lists usually derive from international treaties or regimes of major suppliers to ensure international coordination and a fair playing field for exporters. The development of common lists is one of the core elements of international cooperation in export controls and is a recommendation under UNSCR 1540. Furthermore, lists are part of several UN and other sanctions regimes.

Licensing policies and procedures. Clear procedures are necessary for exporters when applying for a license to export an item on the control list, as well as for regulators in authorizing or denying applications. Procedures include mechanisms to analyze proposed end-uses and end-users, assess risk of diversion, evaluate compatibility of the exports with the overall foreign and security policy of the country, and share information between technical, intelligence and policy experts in governmental agencies. In some cases, one single government entity concentrates licensing responsibilities, such as Germany. Other systems, such as the United States, distribute responsibilities across different agencies and in cases such as Belgium, there are different subnational entities. Licensing procedures must include clear mechanisms to ensure the confidentiality of the information provided by the exporter to the authority.

Enforcement and prosecution procedures. Agencies responsible for enforcement of export control regulations must have the legal authority and the adequate training and technologies to examine exports and identify cases of non-compliance and violations. Efficient inter-governmental cooperation mechanisms are important in order to support adequate information-sharing mechanisms, analysis of relevant data, ensure appropriate record-keeping and other risk assessment strategies. An effective system may require procedures to confirm that exports reach their intended end-user and end-use and that they remain there.

The role of industry. Additionally, an export control system is only efficient if the exporters (companies, researchers, etc.) are aware of their requirements under export control regulations and are capable of complying adequately with such procedures, which often tend to be complex. Export control systems must develop comprehensive strategies for reaching out to exporters and explain the rationale of export controls and their operative procedures. Export control systems tend to rely on interaction and information-sharing between the authority and the exporters. This communication must be secure and must ensure that proprietary and confidential information is adequately protected.

While export controls may be seen as a burden by many exporters, they are also a tool which may help companies and researchers protect their intellectual property. Indeed, good cooperation with licensing authorities is a valuable mechanism to prevent diversion of strategic goods and technologies. Compliance with export controls not only ensures that exporters avoid possible legal consequences, it also prevents them from the reputational damage incurred by supporting proliferation programs. Crucially, this can happen also unknowingly, for example with the very recently and widely publicized case of almost 200 British academics under investigation for "unwittingly helping the Chinese government build weapons of mass destruction" [16, 17].

International cooperation. Besides developing their own systems of control, those States which produce and supply most strategic goods and technologies have different incentives to coordinate their policies and frameworks. They have developed multilateral export control regimes to support each other in their non-proliferation objectives and to reduce the danger of collective action problems in the manner of economic undercuts by putting in place mechanisms that dissuade partners from authorizing exports which have been previously denied by another partner [18]. This coordination relies on a secure exchange of highly sensitive information, an area where DLT can provide the highest standards. Export controls are also an essential component of bilateral mechanisms such as nuclear cooperation agreements (NCAs), which create the framework for civil nuclear cooperation between countries, incorporate specific conditions of supply and entail sharing of information, knowledge, or material resources related to nuclear power technologies (Fig. 1).

Throughout the Cold War, export controls were associated with the most technologically advanced countries and in many ways, they still are. However, the UNSC resolution 1540, adopted in 2004, mandated all States to establish, develop, review, and maintain appropriate effective national export and trans-shipment controls over materials related to nuclear, chemical, or biological weapons, and their means of delivery. Thus, UNSC resolution 1540 represents a fundamental step towards the universalization of export controls as a tool to prevent the proliferation of WMD, particularly with a view to stopping non-state actors from acquiring such weapons. As a growing number of States seek to develop export control systems and come to terms with the growing challenges of striking a balance between permitting legitimate trade while protecting sensitive supply chains, as well as detecting exports of concern while handling proprietary information, the relevance of DLT as a tool that may enable easier and better implementation will become increasingly evident.

The trend towards universalization of export controls can also be seen in the field of conventional arms. The Arms Trade Treaty (ATT) which includes controls on export, import, transit, trans-shipment and brokering of arms, opened for signature in 2013 and has been ratified by more than 100 States. As global adoption of export controls grows, their effective implementation will be increasingly important to reduce a

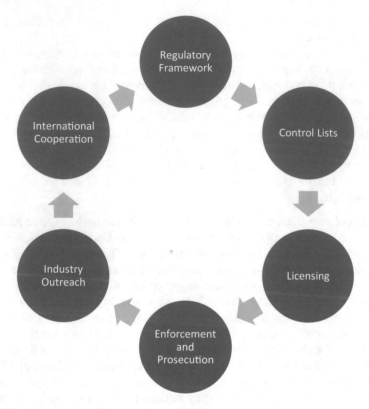

Fig. 1 Effective export controls

loophole in the international security architecture by ensuring the integrity of strategic supply chains and diminishing the risk of diversion of critical items.[3]

DLT offers considerable opportunities to manage information in a secure and transparent way and to support the tracking of sensitive items, making implementation of export controls easier and more secure. In this regard, it is a promising technology for States seeking to develop and set in motion their export control systems, but also for those with already existing systems but who regularly seek to modernize and increase their efficiency.

---

[3] The current architecture includes the Wassenaar Arrangement, which promotes transparency and greater responsibility in transfers of conventional arms and dual-use goods and technologies, thus preventing destabilizing accumulations; the Zangger Committee, which serves as the "faithful interpreter" of Article III.2 of the Treaty on the Proliferation of Nuclear Weapons (NPT), to harmonize the interpretation of nuclear export control policies for NPT Parties; the Nuclear Suppliers Group, which contributes to the non-proliferation of nuclear weapons through the implementation of two sets of Guidelines for nuclear exports and nuclear-related exports; the Australia Group, which seeks to ensure that exports do not contribute to the development of chemical or biological weapons; and the Missile Technology Control Regime, which aims at preventing proliferation of unmanned delivery systems capable of delivering weapons of mass destruction.

3 Challenges in Export Controls

The need to secure and streamline information exchange among parties is an important challenge for achieving efficient export controls. Additionally, governments need to have technical experts who are capable of classifying and identifying controlled items in order to properly implement the control lists in the different fields such as military, nuclear, chemical or biological. Procedures for technical experts to interact with licensing authorities and with customs and border authorities must also be in place in order to assess risk and evaluate exports of concern. This is particularly relevant in those cases where these experts work in non-government or non-central government institutions, raising additional consideration regarding the exchange of confidential or proprietary information. In fact, fluent interaction between government agencies in order to review delicate license applications is essential for a well-functioning licensing system. A licensing process includes the sequence of steps for interagency consultation and decision-making procedures in analyzing specific requests [19] and in many cases there are multiple licensing agencies distributed between different governmental authorities or even between different levels of government. These coordination mechanisms usually entail setting up adequate mechanisms for information exchange and analyzing and evaluating information contained in databases and lists that different agencies possess (pre-approved entities and end-users, end-users of concern, trade statistics, embargoes, watchlists, etc.).

Governments must not only design mechanisms for licensing authorities to access, evaluate, and exchange secure data from different agencies, they must also find ways of processing large amounts of data and paperwork derived from a high number of applications, which can be a burdensome activity for many governments and where DLT can interact with other technologies quite efficiently. For example, in the United States, the Bureau of Industry and Security (BIS) reviewed a total of 34,851 license applications for dual-use items in 2018, a notable increase from around 22,000 in 2010 [20]. In the EU, statistical estimates of the relative importance of dual-use trade in 2018 indicate that dual-use exports represented about 2.3% of EU total exports (intra and extra-EU), reaching a total value of EUR 50.2 billion [21].

A license application must be supported by a considerable set of documents with information on the item itself as well as on the proposed end-use and end-user. Proving the validity of these documents is important for licensing authorities and, when violations are detected, for prosecutors. Enforcement officers must have the legal and technical tools, as well as the training, to investigate, detect, and prosecute violations. A good number of proven violations of export controls are tied to complex mechanisms and constructions of front companies which enable proliferators to find loopholes in the supply chain, often taking advantage of critical points such as transit and trans-shipment ports, where a considerable amount of operations may take place on a regular basis, or through the presence of brokers [22, 23].

A statement by the exporter is not always enough to obtain certainty about the final destination of a product. Even if the documents provided are truthful and reliable, the integrity of the supply chain may be broken by further diversion or re-export of the original export. Licenses are very often issued with specific conditions attached, which often refer to mechanisms to prove that the good or technology remains with its stated end-user after the export took place. Some governments are beginning to implement post-shipment verifications to certify this and further strengthen these efforts. Governments also find it particularly challenging to implement and enforce controls over intangible transfers of technology (so-called ITT controls). Ensuring that dissemination of technologies and know-how does not contribute to proliferation is essential to guarantee the integrity of supply chains, which explains why universities and researchers are critical exporters.

As already discussed, export controls require fluent and effective interaction between exporters and authorities, which include exchange of information at several stages. DLT ensures that this exchange is conducted in an orderly, transparent, secure and auditable way, mitigating the likelihood that corrupt schemes take place. According to a recent study on challenges for export control implementation in the European Union, the authorities have sought to reduce the administrative burden associated with the implementation of export controls, while placing more responsibility for their implementation on the companies [11]. This highlights the need for adequate, transparent, and reliable modes of interaction between them.

On the other hand, exporters themselves face several challenges which may be: (1) technical, such as properly identifying and understanding the control lists; (2) administrative, especially related to the complex procedures for obtaining licenses and providing all the required information about an export and the proposed end uses and end users; (3) legal, regarding the capacity to correctly understand what may often be complex legislation and secondary regulations; and (4) logistical, including the capacity to monitor and track items across complex supply chains and in different jurisdictions as well as to assess the risk of a specific export by identifying 'red flags' such as prohibited or suspicious parties, end-users, end-uses, or illicit trafficking routes [11].

Governments have begun to develop technological solutions to help exporters tackle some of these challenges. Several governments are moving into e-based licensing systems, where the interaction between government and exporters is conducted online. The Republic of Korea has turned to applications of artificial intelligence to cope with the growing challenge of managing large volumes of data in processing applications [24] and governments have developed platforms which help companies properly identify and classify potentially controlled items[4] [25] and there are a number of software tools available to help companies perform certain elements of risk assessments [26].

---

[4] In the US, BIS has developed the Simplified Network Application Process-Redesign (SNAP-R) which allows companies to submit a production classification request for dual-use goods.

4 Potential Applications of DLT to the Implementation of Effective Export Controls

While the trend towards technological support in export controls has begun, little attention has been given to the way in which DLT could help with some of the challenges previously identified and the ways in which it would do so better than other technologies [7]. This shows, as Cindy Vestergaard highlighted in the Introduction to this volume, that the culture of international security often lies in contrast to the rapid pace of the innovation culture. The lack of attention to DLT is surprising given the growing number of blockchain applications already under way in sectors such as government processes, waste management, identification, border controls, healthcare, music, or supply chains [27].

Supply chain management and identity management have been particularly emphasized as potentially successful uses of blockchain. A recent study suggests that industry and governments can apply this technology in problems when shared governance, verifiable state and/or resilience to data loss are necessary. It shows that DLT can support tracking valuable material assets that are distributed globally when provenance is an important consideration, for example diamonds, works of art, certified goods, or items which change hands several times over long distances, as well as individual components of assembled devices. It suggests its capacity to establish the source of each part that has been used to identify a maintenance history are particularly useful for heavily regulated industries such as airlines, and for military/intelligence applications [28]. There are several interesting examples of this, such as Everledger, which has a blockchain system to provide secure proof of origin and sourcing of goods such as diamonds, wine, and art.

Furthermore, identities and the properties for those identities can be maintained on a DLT system. The ability of a DLT platform to store documents and information about these documents is of particular relevance for records that are highly valuable, such as certificates and government licenses [28]. A report by the World Bank found that DLT can be useful in a wide variety of sectors which face similar challenges to the ones that have been identified for export controls [4].[5]

Taking into consideration the biggest challenges faced by export controls practitioners and the strengths of DLT, this chapter identifies three concrete use cases to improve implementation of export controls: (1) sensitive data management and licensing processes; (2) detection and prevention of falsified documents and valid identities; and (3) traceability of sensitive items.

---

[5] These include: managing digital identity platforms; management of inventory and disputes in supply chain management; product provenance and authenticity (e.g. artworks, pharmaceuticals, diamonds); trade finance; post-trade processing; intellectual property registration; e-voting systems; e-residence; government record-keeping, e.g. criminal records; reducing fraud and error in government payments; and reducing tax fraud and protection of critical infrastructure against cyberattacks.

4.1 Sensitive Data Management and Licensing Processes

Data transferred between companies in the supply chain, between companies and governments, within governments, and between different governments includes proprietary and sometimes classified information and must be protected from cyber-attacks and from insider theft as securely as possible. In this interlocking set of data exchanges, governments have an interest in protecting policy sensitive data, while companies and researchers also have an interest in securing this information ("trans-actions") in order to protect their intellectual and commercial property, including technical specifications and also pricing information. A core advantage of permis-sioned DLT systems is to better monitor transactions while allowing for adequate protection of proprietary information and access controls to that information [6]. This makes DLT particularly suitable in matching core interests of authorities and exporters in export controls.

An official document outlining challenges for export controls in the United States identifies cyber-intrusions and data exfiltration that result in the export of controlled technology as a new area of focus in outreach efforts. It indicates that this theft of export-controlled information is "becoming almost a daily occurrence," posing a considerable threat to national security interests and to the intellectual property of companies [23]. DLT can be a highly effective tool to maintain data integrity and protect information against theft, as any alteration in the process would be visible to everyone in the platform. As transactions and data are recorded and replicated across participants, hackers do not have a single point of entry or single point of attack, nor can they access entire repositories of data if they do get in, thus turning the distributed nature of DLT as a particularly effective tool against cyberattacks [4].

Some governments have begun to develop electronic licensing systems and other advanced technological tools to facilitate the application process, to protect export control information, and to manage the increasing number of documents related to applications. Electronic licensing systems typically have a front office where industry can interact with government, and a back office where government author-ities manage applications and interact with each other. For example, Estonia has developed Stratlink, one of the most advanced e-licensing platforms for strategic goods. The software allows for export permits for dual-use items to be digitized, from applications for licenses up to the point of printing the license. Stratlink significantly reduces the days needed to finalize the process, and additionally offers a transparent strategic goods information system that mitigates corruption and illicit transfers of armaments and dual-use items. Stratlink contains a public side available to all appli-cants and an administrative side available to organizations, officials, and experts responsible for managing export controls. The system allows the submission of applications online, enables communication between exporters and licensing author-ities, and supports storing issued licenses and other documents. At the same time, the licensing officers review license applications and conduct interagency reviews through the system [29].

A DLT-layer to process license applications would potentially provide highly efficient interaction between exporter and authority with an added degree of security regarding the confidentiality of the proprietary information provided in applications. It would enhance the degree to which different government agencies can interact with each other under clearly defined and secure protocols and algorithms which would define the process for governmental interaction, specifying the respective responsibilities and input that each agency can provide to the evaluation of an application, which include revision of potentially large amounts of data [23].

At the same time, posting data on a DLT platform does not mean that the content of the data is readable to everyone, since "keys" associated to digital identities function as permissions which enable specific actors to write and/or read the encrypted information on the DLT. In this way, the records of the exporter become the same as the State record and the national authority has the capacity to define the levels of access that exporters enjoy to certain files. This is useful not just for security but also for auditability since there is one authoritative ledger.

A DLT layer in a licensing system could ensure auditability of internal compliance on export control rules and regulations and relevant exchanges between government and exporter, and to support reporting requirements by exporters, for example in General or Global Licenses.

DLT is a useful tool for effective recordkeeping. Licensing authorities are required to maintain robust and secure records of applications, particularly for cases when decisions are contested at courts. One authoritative ledger would provide the investigation agencies, as well as the exporters, certainty regarding the information contained in the records. These records are also relevant to comply with different international reporting obligations, such as nuclear exports under the International Atomic Energy Agency Additional Protocol, arms exports under the ATT or the UN register of conventional arms, chemical declarations under the Chemical Weapons Convention which is discussed in the previous chapter, or different reports under multilateral export control regimes.

Proprietary information is not only exchanged between private entities and authorities. In the case of some nuclear exports, governments may exchange information through different mechanisms such as those incorporated in nuclear cooperation agreements, which have several bilateral reporting conditions that may be ideally suited for a DLT platform set up between the authorities involved in the process in the two governments. Taking the case of Australia as an example, it can be seen that NCAs stipulate that detailed administrative arrangements are to be concluded between the Australian Safeguards and Non-Proliferation Office, and its counterpart, setting out the procedures to apply in accounting and reporting on nuclear materials [30, 31].[6]

---

[6] For example, the 2018 the Agreement between Australia and the United Kingdom on Cooperation in the Peaceful Uses of Nuclear Energy indicates that parties shall provide reporting of all transfers and receipts, and an annual report on all transactions and inventories, shall take all appropriate precautions to preserve the confidentiality of commercial and other confidential information received, and shall ensure the adequate and effective protection of intellectual property created and technology transferred.

A DLT-based framework to exchange sensitive information bilaterally would aptly complement bilateral agreements and processes ensuring the validity and confidentiality of information and guaranteeing that the two parties have access to the same data. Under clear protocols identifying the responsibilities of each actor, different government agencies (e.g. regulators) and exporters (e.g. facilities) operating under the bilateral framework could be included in the platform in order to integrate the reporting elements from each of the two sides, strengthening the transparency and verification provisions of the bilateral agreements.

4.2   Valid Identities and Detection and Prevention of Falsified Documents

An important task for governments is corroborating the validity of the growing number of documents that are routinely processed and analyzed in export control applications. Forged documents and fake recipients are often used to circumvent export control regulations and support the illicit export of sensitive items, as can be seen in several accounts of cases taken to court in different jurisdictions [22, 23, 26]. A report by BIS shows that the false statements made on an export document or to a federal law enforcement officer indicate that an export is destined for one country when it is really destined for a sanctioned destination; that the export does not require a license when in fact it does; provide false item valuations; or indicate that an export was shipped under a particular license number when in fact that license was for a different item [23].

In light of these challenges, DLT is a particularly effective tool to ensure data integrity and provenance, guaranteeing that digital documents, such as end-use certificates and other documentation provided in an application, have not been falsified. This would equally apply to licenses and permits issued by authorities. DLT achieves this through the creation of hashes in which each transaction is "hashed" with its own digital fingerprint, time-stamped and put on the shared ledger, which in turn is linked (hashed) to previous transactions. The hash is related to a document but the document itself does not need to be put on the ledger; instead, the hash proves that the original transaction took place. The combination of hashing and timestamping makes DLT systems highly tamperevident. By timestamping a document, one can prove when and by whom a transaction was created. Hashing ensures that if anyone attempts to modify or delete information in one block, the subsequent block will reject the mediation [32]. The correlation between physical and digital assets enabled by DLT is useful in order to monitor transactions and track documents more efficiently and in an auditable way, reducing the risk of errors and potentially supporting investigative efforts by prosecutors.

One of the most valuable features of DLT is the creation of digital identities, which are secure certificates whose issuance is enabled by DLT and which provide different actors with appropriate permissions and can also prove who conducted a transaction (who issued a document, who conducted an inspection, who received an item). Documents attached to licensing applications on a DLT platform would be time-stamped, hashed and, therefore, impossible to forge or falsify and their provenance corroborated. While DLT does not prevent actors with permissioned access from entering fraudulent or incorrect data, digital identities could further help by identifying the actor responsible for a transaction, even if this actor may feed the ledger with erroneous or malicious input of incorrect data [6].

Digital identities could be assigned to authorized or pre-approved end-users in a supply chain, as well as to people responsible for export control applications in private entities. Broker validation processes and certificates could also be assigned to authorized brokers to limit the diversion risks associated with such activities. Guaranteeing the validity of documents and identities would considerably improve the efficiency of export control procedures, particularly where the volume of data becomes increasingly difficult to manage such as in transit and trans-shipment ports.

From the point of view of major exporters who routinely apply for export control licenses, a DLT-based solution within their own supply chain could expedite operations and provide assurance to the licensing authority about their end-users. Exporters could make a strong case with licensing authorities about the strength of their own export applications and the integrity of their own supply chain if all the documentation generated throughout the process were put on a DLT platform. In such a process, assigning valid identities to end-users would greatly reduce the risk of fake companies, as any actor on the platform requesting an export would be pre-approved and the possibility to identify that the user is indeed the pre-approved one is enabled by DLT. Furthermore, DLT would also support proper follow-up in case an investigation is needed. Thus, a DLT-based application would greatly support the integrity and validity of the documentation provided to the authority [32]. Two elements of DLT thus mutually reinforce each other to guarantee the validity of documents and entities: data and process integrity. Data integrity is achieved through the time stamp and process integrity shows the steps or order in which things happened based on the rules that must be followed.

Furthermore, a DLT-system within a specific supply chain could be integrated with a DLT-based licensing system, creating a stronger system of interaction between licensing authorities and the extended supply chain actors and enabling the controls to oversee and validate the different transactions that occur in the process [5, 33]. As has already been stressed, this does not mean that every bit of information itself is readable to everyone on the DLT platform. In this case, permissions specified by the licensing authority would indicate which actors could access and/or feed specific information and the process set up ensures that only the holders of the relevant keys can access specific information. This would of course carry considerable challenges in terms of acceptability and also interoperability, but an integrated system could achieve security and immutability on every transaction across the export process (e.g. request for an export between companies, export license application, application evaluation within a government, license authorization and delivery of the export).

A final step in ensuring that the integrity of a supply chain after an export has taken place would be a solid mechanism to verify that the export remains where it was intended to remain, which as we have seen could be a condition added to the license and tied to a smart contract. While this information can be obtained through the verification provided by a post-shipment verification, the next subsection will show that items can be tracked and this information can be added to a DLT platform.

4.3 Traceability of Sensitive Items

A DLT platform could enable the licensing authority and the exporter to maintain oversight of the actual destination of the exported asset. It has been mentioned that supply chain management and tracking the transport of certain goods across borders are some of the best use cases for DLT.

Export controls seek to avoid the diversion of legitimate exports by ensuring that sensitive exports are used for authorized end-uses and by authorized end-users. The effectiveness of the authorizations issued can also be complemented with on-site inspections that take place after the export has occured, the so-called post-shipment controls. DLT could support post-shipment verification by enhancing the efficiency and transparency in tracing specific exports. Authorized personnel (through digital identities) conducting on-site post-shipment verifications could record their observations on a DLT system, ensuring the security and auditability of records.

Technological solutions could further complement these tracing activities to ensure correlation between the physical assets and the digital records. Some producers of machine tools, one of the most export control-relevant dual-use goods, have added transfer detection devices to their products, which transmit real time information on the location of the items. This information could be fed to the DLT platform, providing reliable consistency between off-chain and on-chain assets. Additional information, such as photographic evidence submitted to the blockchain, could further be used to prove the location of an export and ultimately support valuable tools in export controls such as post-shipment verification.

Implementing export controls on intangible assets is one of the most pressing challenges in the efforts to avert proliferation. A recent study by King's College identified the dimension of this challenge and concluded that "a broader strategy is required to control intangible technology transfers that could aid proliferation" [34]. Often researchers and developers of controlled technology are unaware of export control provisions associated with their information, which explains that governments and licensing authorities have increased efforts on conducting outreach to academia and research institutions as a means to counter proliferation threats associated to intangible transfers [35–37]. Recent highly publicized cases may help increase attention to the issue. Researchers and universities have increased their awareness that intangible transfers of technology may not only unwillingly support programs of concern from a proliferation point of view but also that they may be loopholes to lose property rights [38].

DLT is particularly effective for tracking data and technologies. If the controlled technology or information is placed on a DLT platform and exported, the exporter would be able to not only guarantee that it is not altered or stolen, but it would always be possible to know where the information is stored, since any transaction would be evident on the ledger. A possible way in which this could be implemented would be if a licensing authority were to set up an ITT-specific DLT platform which would enable the export of controlled technologies and keys to access the actual technology could be shared with authorized end-users, thus enabling the transfer of technology under a supervised environment where every transfer of the actual export could be traced. In this way, the final end-user would not be able to transfer the information further without informing the entire platform. This innovative solution would of course apply only to those exporters who would willingly transfer their knowledge or technology in this way. The challenge of expanding this to the vast majority of unknowing or unwilling "academic" exporters remains one of the major probllems facing export controls authorites.

The ability of DLT to provide oversight over the movement of controlled data makes it also an interesting tool to manage and protect "fractional ownership," e.g. rights owned by various holders. This would also be useful to track the individual components of complex assembled devices where the parts have different origins [3]. This would be highly useful in export controls, where a threshold may be set for an allowed percentage of controlled components in an item under the *de minimis* rule. In the U.S., for example, a non-U.S. made item that incorporates controlled U.S. origin content that exceeds a certain de minims percentage is subject to controls [39].

As already mentioned, DLT is particularly useful for maintaining clarity on the provenance of items under global distribution. This is the case, for example, of patented innovations, where development is achieved through collaboration between various individuals and entities, complicating considerably the management of patent rights. The tracing abilities of DLT support the registration and tracking of each contribution and could even, through a smart contract, ensure automatic remuneration. This feature of DLT makes it easier to control and track the distribution of intellectual property, and to manage rights and payments.

From an export control point of view, several strategic items may have individual components with different origins, where each or some of them may be subject to export controls, for example a nuclear reactor. Specific DLT solutions which could be jointly set up by the licensing authority and industry to support the licensing of particularly sensitive items in the nuclear fuel cycle or in certain military projects could be set up to address the specific challenge of provenance and simultaneously protect information and technology associated with the specific project.

5 Conclusion

Distributed ledger technology possesses several characteristics which may increase efficiency, transparency, and security in several global processes and in particular "promise to have far-reaching implications for global trade and supply chains" [5]. These characteristics, such as auditability, resilience, immutability, and capacity to automatize processes, are well suited to increase the effective implementation of export controls, a critical element of the overall non-proliferation regime and of the international security architecture. The sum of these characteristics makes DLT a more promising solution than other digital technologies to support international security efforts.

DLT and blockchain can be expected to become increasingly relevant as tools to improve different aspects of the governance of trade, such as customs management, management of inventory, disputes in supply chain management or trade finance. The potential of DLT to digitize trade and combine actors in trade finance, border procedures, transportation and logistics, financial services, insurance, retail distribution, and government procurement, etc. is particularly promising, because this integration may take place while providing for a secure environment.

There is a growing interest in public–private initiatives to develop digital infrastructure models that would further connect different actors along the supply chain in a more holistic way on a DLT [40]. This would have the potential to transform the world of transportation and logistics. One of the most important challenges for realizing this potential will be related to the interoperability of different platforms or ledgers, particularly assuming that many processes across supply chains may increasingly run on DLT technology.

In export controls, the fluent interaction needed between exporter and authority strengthen the case for shared-governance solutions, but operating under strict protocols identifying responsibilities and protecting information. The potential applications of DLT are enormous and it is not inconceivable that both global trade and security strategies will increasingly apply DLT solutions, which would open the door for integrated approaches in export controls. Export controls must keep pace with the expected technological revolution in general trade processes through increased efficiency, transparency and security. As trade becomes more digitalized and automatized, export controls will need to "keep up" in order to continue to identify potential shipments of concern without disrupting legitimate trade and becoming an unduly burden for companies.

We are far away from knowing for certain the degree to which fully integrated scenarios will become reality, as well as the way in which public and private actors will be ready to manage sensitive information through novel technological solutions based on distributed ledgers. The viability of these efforts will depend on the success of specific projects and on the capacity to integrate targeted initiatives. This chapter has argued that DLT could support export control implementation through at least three possible ways: (1) sensitive data management and licensing processes; (2) valid identities and detection and prevention of falsified documents; and (3) traceability of sensitive items.

Looking beyond issues associated with the implementation of export controls, it is pertinent to mention that ensuring the continued functionality, neutrality, and focus of this area of the non-proliferation regime will become increasingly important as more countries adopt regulatory frameworks conducive to strategic controls. The capacity of the non-proliferation community to achieve this will increase the global legitimacy of export controls as a valuable tool in the creation of a more secure international community.

References

1. Collins C, Frantz D (2018) The long shadow of A.Q. Khan: how one scientist helped the world go nuclear. https://www.foreignaffairs.com/articles/north-korea/2018-01-31/long-shadow-aq-khan. Accessed 28 May 2021
2. Fitzpatrick M (2007) Nuclear black markets: Pakistan, A.Q. Khan and the rise of proliferation networks—a net assessment. The International Institute for Strategic Studies, London
3. Emmanuelle G (2018) Can blockchain revolutionize international trade?, 1st edn. World Trade Organization Publications, Geneva. https://www.wto.org/english/res_e/booksp_e/blockc hainrev18_e.pdf. Accessed 28 May 2021
4. World Bank Group (2017) Distributed ledger technology (DLT) and blockchain. FinTech Note (1). http://documents.worldbank.org/curated/en/177911513714062215/pdf/122140-WP-PUB LIC-Distributed-Ledger-Technology-and-Blockchain-Fintech-Notes.pdf. Accessed 28 May 2021
5. World Economic Forum (2019) White paper: inclusive deployment of blockchain for supply chains: part 1 introduction. http://www3.weforum.org/docs/WEF_Introduction_to_Blockc hain_for_Supply_Chains.pdf. Accessed 28 May 2021
6. Angert S (2019) Blockchain technology implementation in the U.S. customs environment. Thesis. Naval Postgraduate School, Monterey California
7. Coscarella C, Minotti A (2020) An institutional blockchain as a tool to control the export of dual-use and military goods. Strat Trade Rev 6(9):93–112
8. Dill CB, Stewart I (2015) Defining effective strategic trade controls at the national level. Strat Trade Rev 1(1):4–17
9. BAFA, Federal Office of Economics and Export Control (2020) Objectives of export control. https://www.bafa.de/EN/Foreign_Trade/Export_Control/export_control_node.html. Accessed 28 May 2021
10. Global Affairs Canada (2017) Export controls handbook. Amended August 2017. https://www.international.gc.ca/controls-controles/assets/pdfs/documents/Export-Controls-Han dbook-2017-eng.pdf. Accessed 04 June 2021
11. Bauer S et al (2017) Challenges and good practices in the implementation of the EU's arms and dual-use export controls: a cross-sector analysis. Stockholm International Peace Research Institute, Solna, Sweden
12. Bureau of Industry and Security (2020) Deemed exports. https://www.bis.doc.gov/index.php/policy-guidance/deemed-exports. Accessed 28 May 2021
13. Achilleas P (2017) Introduction export control. In: Dai T, Achilleas P (eds) Theory and practice of export control; balancing international security and international economic relations, Kobe University Social Science Research Series. Springer, Singapore, p 4
14. Congressional Research Service (2020) The U.S. export control system and the export control reform initiative (R41916). https://fas.org/sgp/crs/natsec/R41916.pdf. Accessed 28 May 2021

15. Asia-Pacific Economic Cooperation (2004) Key elements for effective export control systems (Ref.: 2004/AMM/036) In: Ministry of Economy, Trade and Industry Japan. https://www.meti.go.jp/policy/anpo/kanri/bouekikanri/kokusaidoko/0322APECdocument.pdf. Accessed 28 May 2021

16. The Export Compliance Journal (2017) End user statements: avoiding export compliance overkill. https://www.visualcompliance.com/blog/?p=470. Accessed 10 June 2021

17. Dathan M (2021) Hundreds of UK academics investigated over weapons links to China. The Times. https://www.thetimes.co.uk/article/hundreds-of-uk-academics-investigated-over-weapons-links-to-china-bpcks76bv. Accessed 28 May 2021

18. Joyner D (2006) Introduction. In: Joyner D (ed) Non-proliferation export controls, origins, challenges, and proposals for strengthening. Ashgate, p 2

19. BAFA, Federal Office of Economics and Export Control (2013) Brief outline on export controls: licensing requirements, application procedure, information sources

20. Bureau of Industry and Security (2018) Statistics of 2018 BIS license authorization. https://www.bis.doc.gov/index.php/documents/technology-evaluation/ote-data-portal/licensing-analysis/2453-2018-statistical-analysis-of-bis-licensing-pdf-1/file. Accessed 28 May 2021

21. European Commission (2019) Report from the Commission to the European Parliament and the Council on the implementation of Regulation (EC) No 428/2009. Brussels, 4.11.2019 COM(2019) 562 final. https://ec.europa.eu/transparency/regdoc/rep/1/2019/EN/COM-2019-562-F1-EN-MAIN-PART-1.PDF. Accessed 28 May 2021

22. Bauer S (2013) WMD-Related dual-use trade control offences in the European Union: penalties and prosecutions. EU Non-Proliferation Consortium. Non-Proliferation Papers, No. 30

23. Bureau of Industry and Security (2020) Don't let this happen to you! Actual investigations of export control and antiboycott violations. https://www.bis.doc.gov/index.php/documents/enforcement/1005-don-t-let-this-happen-to-you-1/file. Accessed 04 June 2021

24. Stanley-Lockman Z (2018) Learning from South Korea: how artificial intelligence can transform US export controls. Bulletin of the Atomic Scientists. https://thebulletin.org/2018/11/learning-from-south-korea-how-artificial-intelligence-can-transform-us-export-controls/. Accessed 28 May 2021

25. Bureau of Industry and Security (2020) Simplified network application process-redesign. https://www.bis.doc.gov/index.php/licensing/simplified-network-application-process-redesign-snap-r. Accessed 28 May 2021

26. Bauer S, Bromley M (2019) Detecting, investigating and prosecuting export control violations: European perspectives on key challenges and good practices. Stockholm International Peace Research Institute, Stockholm

27. Zago M (2018) 50+ examples of how blockchains are taking over the world. Medium. https://medium.com/@matteozago/50-examples-of-how-blockchains-are-taking-over-the-world-4276bf488a4b. Accessed 28 May 2021

28. Ruoti S et al (2019) Blockchain technology: what is it good for? Industry's dreams and fears for this new technology. Association for Computing Machinery (ACM) Queue (17) 5. https://queue.acm.org/detail.cfm?id=3376896. Accessed 28 May 2021

29. Plantera F (2018) An Estonian software could be the ultimate enemy of corruption and arms smuggling. E-estonia. https://e-estonia.com/estonian-software-ultimate-enemy-corruption-arms-smuggling/. Accessed 28 May 2021

30. Carlson J (2006) The role of bilateral nuclear safeguards agreements. Trust Verify 122:1–4

31. Australasian Legal Information Institute (2018) Agreement between the Government of Australia and the Government of the United Kingdom of Great Britain and Northern Ireland on cooperation in the peaceful uses of nuclear energy. Canberra. http://www.austlii.edu.au/au/other/dfat/treaties/ATS/2021/1.html. Accessed 28 May 2021

32. Thevoz P (2020) Blockchain and the traceability of critical materials. In: Conference at the Stimson Center, Washington D.C. 2020. https://www.youtube.com/watch?v=IURN4oTdRBM. Accessed 16 Feb 2020. Accessed 28 May 2021

33. Schulte S et al (2019) Towards blockchain interoperability. In: Di Ciccio C et al (eds) Business process management: blockchain and Central and Eastern Europe forum, BPM 2019 Blockchain and CEE Forum, Vienna, Austria. https://www.infosys.tuwien.ac.at/team/sschulte/paper/2019_SSFB19_BPM_BF.pdf. Accessed 28 May 2021
34. Stewart I (2016) Project Alpha at King's College London Part 2: case studies. King's College London, London. https://www.kcl.ac.uk/csss/assets/itt-case-studies-part-2-1.pdf. Accessed 28 May 2021
35. BAFA, Federal Office of Economics and Export Control (2019) Export control and academia manual. Druckhaus Berlin-Mitte GmbH, Berlin
36. METI Ministry of Economy, Trade and Industry (2018) METI launches e-learning program in academic and research institutes in the field of security export control. https://www.meti.go.jp/english/press/2018/0529_003.html. Accessed 28 May 2021
37. Public Safety Canada (2019) Safeguarding science. https://www.publicsafety.gc.ca/cnt/ntnl-scrt/cntr-trrrsm/cntr-prlfrtn/index-en.aspx. Accessed 28 May 2021
38. Starks B, Tucker C (2017) Export control compliance and American academia. Strat Trade Rev 3:69–79
39. Cook S, Kook N (2015) De minimis and direct product rules. Bureau of Industry and Security. https://bis.doc.gov/index.php/documents/licensing-forms/1408-condensed-pdf-presentation-slides-16-dec-2015pm/file. Accessed 28 May 2021
40. Costa D et al (2019) Quadrans white paper rev.01. Quadrans Foundation. https://quadrans.io/content/files/quadrans-white-paper-rev01.pdf. Accessed 28 May 2021